Writing Ancient History

Writing Ancient History

Neville Morley

Cornell University Press
Ithaca, New York

First published 1999 by Cornell University Press.

Library of Congress Cataloging-in-Publication Data

Morley, Neville
  Writing ancient history / Neville Morley.
    p. cm.
  Includes bibliographical references (p.) and index.
  ISBN 0-8014-8633-5
  1. History, Ancient—Historiography. I. Title.
  D56.M66 1999
  930'.07'2—dc21   99-28001

Printed in Great Britain

For my parents
Yes, this is what I do for a living

Contents

Acknowledgements   9
Introduction   11

1. What is History?   19

2. The Use and Abuse of Sources   53

3. Telling the Story   97

4. What is History *For*?   133

Epilogue   163
Further Reading   165
Index   173

Acknowledgements

With the express purpose of locating myself within existing academic networks and hierarchies, I should like to thank all the teachers who, wittingly or not, led me to think about the ways in which I should go about writing history: Peter Burke (Cambridge), Paul Cartledge (Cambridge), Peter Garnsey (Cambridge), Keith Hopkins (Cambridge), Paul Millett (anyone noticed a pattern yet?), Gwyn Prins (guess) and Jonathan Walters (formerly Cambridge, anyway). I have of course benefited greatly from conversations with my colleagues at Bristol, especially John Betts, Catharine Edwards, Duncan Kennedy, Charles Martindale, Ellen O'Gorman and Vanda Zajko. On a tantalisingly vague personal note, I must thank Anne, for everything as usual; Angharad and Owain; and Boris and Basil, without whom the experience of writing this book might have been shorter but would certainly have been less interesting. However, my greatest debt is to the students of Lampeter and Bristol who sat, more or less bemused and befuddled, through all my desperate attempts to explain that historical theory really *matters* . . .

Bristol, 1999 N.M.

Introduction

I shall offer a little advice and these few precepts to the
historians, so that I may share in their building project, if not
the inscription on it, by touching the clay with my finger-tip.
And yet most of them think they have no need of advice for
the job, any more than they need a set of rules for walking or
seeing or eating, but they think it is perfectly simple and easy
to write history, if only someone can express clearly what
occurs to them …. Therefore I know that I shall not convert
very many of them: I shall seem a great nuisance to some,
particularly to anyone whose history is already finished and
has already been displayed in public.
> Lucian (*c.* AD 115-80), author of a wide range of (for
> the most part satirical) speeches, dialogues, stories,
> letters and essays, including this one:
> *How To Write History,* 4-5

How do ancient historians 'do' ancient history? At one end
of the process, there is a miscellaneous assortment of material – coins, pieces of pottery, inscriptions, remains of buildings, works of art and above all literary texts of various kinds
– that has survived, more or less accidentally, from antiquity.
At the other end, we find that this material has been trans-

formed into books and articles that claim to be able to tell
you all about different aspects of life in the ancient world.
This book aims to discuss various questions that might be
asked about this process of transformation: How exactly do
ancient historians go about reconstructing and representing
the past? How far can their reconstructions be trusted? How
does history differ from other sorts of writing about the past?
Why do we bother trying to learn about history? Finally
(since I think it's possible to identify some flaws in current
practice), how *should* we write ancient history?

These questions seem to me to be entirely obvious and
straightforward. The *answers* to them may be rather more
complicated and controversial, but the problem of how to
'do' ancient history, how to recover the past from its few
scattered remnants, is surely one that should concern every
ancient historian, from students to professors. However, in
my experience such issues are rarely discussed among professional ancient historians, let alone raised with their students.
People embarking on degree courses in ancient history are
for the most part left to find their own way into the subject
through a process of trial and error, attempting to produce
work that satisfies their teachers by imitating the approaches
of the books they find on their reading lists. If they are given
any explicit guidance at all, it tends to be little more than a
homily on the importance of basing their arguments on the
sources (or at any rate mentioning the odd piece of ancient
evidence in their essays). The unspoken assumption of much
ancient history teaching, and still more of the sort of books

that are usually set as Introductions to Ancient History, is that historical writing is a 'natural' activity that does not need to be taught or even thought about.

Things are little different among the lecturers and professors, the 'proper', fully fledged ancient historians. After all, these are the people who were, as students, most adept at mimicking the accepted style and approach of ancient history as it was understood by their teachers. One generation thus passes its indifference to historical theory on to the next. Ancient historians argue endlessly about different interpretations of the ancient evidence, but they treat the *act* of interpretation, the move from evidence to reconstruction, as simple and unproblematic. Questions of theory and methodology are regarded as pointless distractions from the business of actually doing history. Worse, such questions may even be perceived as a threat to the subject, as if any examination of the ways in which ancient historians write about the past will inevitably undermine the authority of their accounts.

Well, perhaps they do have a point there. While I take a certain nervous pride in the idea that I may be thought a great nuisance for investigating such issues, I can also understand why some historians regard historical theory with hostility. No one wants to be told that his book, the fruit of years of research, writing, obsession and heartache, has fundamental methodological flaws (even if, from one point of view, it's the author's own fault for ignoring such problems in the first place). No one wants to be told that her way of doing history is wrong, that she's put all her effort into imitating models

that aren't worth imitating. Most writers on historical theory
would agree that it is impossible to produce a completely
objective picture of 'how it really was' in the past, untainted
by the historian's preconceptions and personality. Such a
conclusion might indeed seem to undermine the authority of
historical accounts and render the whole enterprise pointless.

Nevertheless, I feel that the issues discussed in this book
are both so obvious and so obviously fundamental that they
can't simply be ignored. I myself don't believe that historical
theory means the death of ancient history; but if for some
reason it did – or if your reading of my argument leads you
to this conclusion – surely this is something that should be
admitted rather than swept under the carpet? An attitude of
indifference or hostility to theory serves very well to maintain
a status quo in which ancient historians can continue to
practise their craft in the traditional manner. However, it
does little for the credibility of the subject among practitioners of more theoretically sophisticated disciplines. Finally, I
at least find the study of historiography a fascinating subject
in its own right, besides what it can tell us about the ways in
which we should be practising what some historians might
call 'proper' ancient history.

In the first chapter I examine the old problem of the
definition of history, 'proper' or otherwise. Historians from
Herodotus and Thucydides onwards have been concerned to
distinguish their own work from other sorts of writing about
the past, such as myths, novels and propaganda. As well as
examining the kinds of answers they have given to the

question 'what is history?', we should consider what is at stake in the drawing of such distinctions, and how far they can be sustained.

In Chapter 2 I turn to the crucial question of the use and abuse of the sources on which historians base their recon-structions of the past. Traditionally, it has been argued that the role of the historian is to leave the facts to 'speak for themselves' without imposing anachronistic theories or per-sonal prejudices on them; only thus is it possible to discover 'how it really was' in the past. However, facts *don't* speak for themselves. The facts have to be identified, selected, trans-lated, interpreted and contextualised *by the historian* before we can learn anything from them; they acquire meaning only when incorporated into the historian's framework of inter-pretation. All of this should lead to a more realistic appraisal of historians' ability to show 'how it really was'. Every work of history is a work of personal interpretation, which can rarely be proved absolutely wrong and never proved abso-lutely right but only found more or less convincing or unconvincing by different readers.

In the third chapter I discuss various aspects of the ways in which historians represent the past, considering (in the words of Hayden White, a key writer on this subject) the historical text as a literary artifact. The impact of a historical account on its readers is only partly dependent on its content. The form of the account – its narrative structure, its style, even its appearance on the page – also plays a part in persuading the reader to accept the historian's version of events. In this chapter I consider the role of narrative in historical writing, the implications of the sort of language that historians commonly use (for example, the use of the impersonal third person passive – 'It is self-evident that ...' – to present the writer's opinions as incontrovertible fact) and the possibilities for introducing new techniques of representation into historiography.

In the final chapter, I examine some of the arguments that have been put forward to justify the practice of history. Why should the state (or parents, for that matter) fund this apparently unproductive activity – does it contribute to the nation's economic well-being, or promote social cohesion, or help us anticipate future events? Why is the past important to people, and why do some people become so fascinated by it that they choose to study history? I argue that the past is of enormous importance for people's sense of personal, social and national identity, and thus the critical study of the past is directly relevant to many debates within contemporary society. However, this may still not fully explain why we find history so fascinating.

One final point. I hope it will be clear that these are my ideas (or my interpretation of other people's ideas), no more and no less. One of the things that I hope you will take away from this book is an awareness of the need to read modern writers ('secondary sources') as critically as you read the ancient evidence, and this one should be no exception. Believe me, all writers are trying to sell you a line. My main aim here is to persuade you of the need to take the issues raised by historical theory seriously; I am far less concerned about whether you then accept my position on those issues. In the (alarming) absence of much other work on the subject, I hope that this book will be a starting-point for your own experiments in writing ancient history.

CHAPTER 1

What is History?

The problem of definition

Any dictionary will give you a range of possible definitions and shades of meaning of the word 'history': just consider the different ways the word is being used in phrases like 'natural history', 'medical history' and 'you're history'. Even in the context of the classroom or lecture theatre the word is ambiguous, meaning both the past and the study of the past. 'Ancient history' is both the sum total of events and processes that took place during a particular period (of history ...) and an academic discipline that involves the study of those events; it is both something that you learn about, and something that you do. History is clearly always concerned in some way with what happened in the past, but not all accounts of the past are considered to be history: what about historical novels, or legends such as that of King Arthur? What about 'pseudo-history' like *The Holy Blood and the Holy Grail* or the works of Erich von Däniken, which claim to be critical accounts of the past but which are, in the eyes of most historians, clearly not 'proper' history? The problem of definition, of determining exactly what history 'is', thus forms the

traditional starting point for studies of the theory and philosophy of history.

Even so, as far as many people are concerned (many
professional historians among them) this really isn't much of
a problem. After all, most words have a number of different
meanings, and usually it's perfectly clear what they mean
from the context in which they're used. The fact that Shake-
speare occasionally used 'history' as a verb does not mean
that there is some fatal ambiguity and uncertainty in the idea
of history as studied in schools and universities. Even the
confusion between history as the past and history as the
study of the past seems rather trivial. 'History' as a subject
covers both: we study a period of history so as to learn how
to do history, and we learn how to do history so as to learn
about different periods of history. We are perfectly well
aware that when we 'write history' we are producing an
account of the past, not reproducing the past itself; there is
no real confusion there. Common sense helps us to distinguish between a proper work of history and a historical
novel, or the ravings of conspiracy theorists and UFOlogists.
Quite simply, we *know* what history is, without the need for
an elaborate theoretical definition; we can recognise it when
we see it.

The fact that I've chosen to follow tradition by devoting
my opening chapter to the problem of definition should
make it clear enough that I think there are some problems
with this 'common sense' approach. Certainly we 'know'
what history is, and can generally recognise it without much

difficulty, but that is not because we are born with some innate historical instinct. On the contrary, it is because we have learnt to understand the word in a certain way, to accept the particular idea of history prevalent in our culture and above all the model of history offered to us by our teachers. The 'common sense' approach to definition assumes that this idea of history, which we acquire more or less unconsciously, is obvious, natural and universally valid. It is taken for granted, not subjected to any analysis or criticism. Each generation of history students learns to follow the unwritten rules laid down by previous generations – often, I suspect, without noticing how far their freedom of thought is being restricted. 'Proper' history is seen to be that which is accepted as such by 'proper' historians – basically, those with university appointments – and most investigations of the nature and methodology of history focus exclusively on the activities of professional historians. History is what historians do: this is a recipe for conservatism if ever there was one.

Even a brief survey of the history of historiography shows clearly that our idea of history is not universally valid but is on the contrary no more and no less than *our* idea. From the time of its invention in the late sixth century BC until the eighteenth century AD, history was regarded as primarily a type of literature. In the nineteenth century it became an academic discipline based in the universities, and was promoted as a kind of science. Different periods have had different ideas of the proper content of history (the idea that historians might study the lower classes, or women, is of

fairly recent date), its methodology (even the earliest historians, like Herodotus and Thucydides, disagreed on the proper
way to treat evidence) and its purpose. History has been
practised in different ways in the past, and it seems either
naive or arrogant to assume that our present methods will
never be improved on in future. If we think of history purely
in terms of its present form, we exclude from consideration
a whole range of possible ideas about what history is and how
it should be practised. It may turn out that this is the correct
thing to do; conceivably, our idea of history *is* far superior to
that of earlier periods, and the activities of present-day professional historians do constitute the highest and/or the
truest form of history yet developed. I have my doubts about
this, and it is certainly not something that we should take for
granted.

Examining our vague, unreasoned assumptions about the
nature of history with a critical eye is not, therefore, a matter
of complicating a perfectly straightforward issue with un-
necessary theorising; it is an indispensable first step in
understanding how to do ancient history. However, the
problem of the definition of history can be understood in
two ways: there is the problem of determining what history
is, and the problem of the act of definition itself. The purpose
of definition is to set up boundaries and limits, above all
between history and other ways of talking about the past.
Definition seeks to privilege certain kinds of writing and to
exclude others from the category of 'proper history'. Osten-
sibly, this is for the sake of convenience, to ensure that the

discussion covers everything that is essential and doesn't bother with inessential or irrelevant matters. In practice, the decision on what is to be considered essential is always a matter of opinion, and it is always, I think, connected to issues of power and authority. There is no such thing as a neutral, unproblematic definition of history; all definitions are working to someone's advantage at someone else's expense. To the question 'What is history?', we must always add: 'Who decides? On what grounds, and to what end?'

The invention of history

I do not think that one will be far wrong in accepting the conclusions which I have reached from the evidence which I have put forward. It is better evidence than that of the poets, who exaggerate the importance of their themes, or of the logographers, who are less interested in telling the truth than in catching the attention of their public, whose authorities cannot be checked and whose subject-matter, owing to the passage of time, is mostly lost in the unreliable streams of mythology. We may claim instead to have used only the plainest evidence and to have reached conclusions which are reasonably accurate, considering that we have been dealing with ancient history ....

And with regard to my factual reporting of the events of the war I have made it a principle not to write down the first story that came my way, and not even to be guided by my own general impressions; either I was present myself at the events which I have described or else I heard of them from eye-witnesses whose reports I have checked with as much thoroughness as possible. Not that even so the truth was easy

to discover: different eye-witnesses give different accounts of
the same events, speaking out of partiality for one side or the
other or else from imperfect memories. And it may well be
that my history will seem less easy to read because of the
absence in it of a romantic element ....

Thucydides (c. 460-400 BC), 1.21-2

History, like so many other intellectual activities, was invented by the ancient Greeks. The word itself comes from
the Greek *historiai*, inquiries, which Herodotus used as the
title of his account of the wars between Greece and Persia,
written in the mid-fifth century BC. Herodotus is often called
the Father of History (though also the Father of Lies, for his
habit of recording outlandish stories about giant ants and
flying snakes). His work offered the deeds of men, not of
gods or heroes, as a fit subject for study, and he sought to
explain *why* the Greeks and Persians had fought one another
rather than simply describing events. Although by our standards he can sometimes seem naive and credulous, he did
display a critical attitude to his sources: 'So much for what
Persians and Phoenicians say ... I prefer to rely on my own
knowledge, and to point out who it was in actual fact that first
injured the Greeks' (1.5).

The work of Thucydides, writing a generation later, was
still closer to what most modern historians would regard as
proper history. He explicitly noted his intention of assessing
the credibility of different sources and rejecting the fabulous
in search of a true account of past events. Thucydides excluded the supernatural altogether from his account,

explaining everything by reference to human actions and
intentions, where Herodotus had left some scope for divine
intervention in the course of events. Finally, Thucydides
established that the proper subjects of historical enquiry
should be war and politics, whereas his predecessor had
included lengthy passages on ethnography, geography, natural history and climatology as well.

Why the Greeks should suddenly have started to think
about their past in a critical manner, weighing up the plausibility of different stories, is unknown. It is surely connected
in some way to the contemporaneous development of philosophy, the practice of critical enquiry into the nature of
society and the workings of the natural world. Some scholars
have linked both these intellectual innovations to the spread
of literacy, others to the emergence of a new form of political
unit governed by its citizens, the *polis*. Whatever the explanation, and for all the differences in aims and methods between
the Greek historians and those of the modern world, the
writings of Herodotus and especially Thucydides are generally identified as the first examples of history as we
understand it. Before the fifth century, there were only
myths, traditions and lists of the great deeds of kings; thereafter, the past was studied (by some, at least) in a properly
critical, analytical and disinterested manner.

The idea that Thucydides' work is something new and
different is not simply one which modern scholars have
developed – though it suits them to be able to claim a long,
distinguished history and a prestigious founding figure for

their subject. Rather, Thucydides himself emphasised the
novelty of his approach to the past, and argued for its
superiority: people should accept *his* conclusions about what
happened. He gave history a distinctive identity, above all by
contrasting his work with the works of others who had
written about the past. His account is better than that of the
poets (who always exaggerate), or the logographers (who are
more interested in dramatic effect than truth), or popular
tradition (which is simply unreliable). His work might lack a
romantic element, and fine literary technique – but that just
shows that it offers the reader a true, unvarnished record of
events.

Thucydides presented his account as being superior even
to other works of history, above all that of his predecessor.
It is notable that he described his enquiry as a *zetesis* (an
inquiry or investigation) or a *suggraphe* (a writing-down, or
simply 'a book'), not a *historie*, and he implicitly rejected
Herodotus' model of history by choosing to concentrate just
on politics and war. He commented sarcastically about people who are 'inclined to accept the first story they hear', giving
as an example some erroneous beliefs about Sparta which
just happen to appear in Herodotus' account. Since the two
men were writing about different periods of history, their
accounts rarely conflict with one another; indeed, Thucydides began his account where Herodotus left off, taking the
latter's account of the Persian Wars as read. Nevertheless,
despite this implicit compliment to his predecessor's work,
Thucydides was concerned to persuade his readers that he

was the more reliable reporter and that his way of enquiring into past events was more accurate and trustworthy.

This is what is at stake in the question 'what is history?', whatever the detail of the answer. 'History' is contrasted with other ways of talking about the past, such as myth, fiction or even other kinds of history, so as to establish it as the preferred way of talking about the past. Differences are emphasised, similarities are ignored. History is contrasted with myth; myth is associated with the fabulous, hence history becomes associated with the real. In time, the idea that history is a true (as opposed to mythical, or fictional) account of the past becomes fixed in people's minds. It then becomes vitally important to decide what is and isn't history, what is and isn't to be recognised as having the prestige and authority of a historical account. It is also important that the boundary between history and other sorts of account should be seen to be clear and unbridgeable, for fear of calling into question history's claim to sole authority over the past. This is not to say that there *are* no differences between these different ways of talking about the past – we shall be examining some of them in the course of this chapter – but the differences may be exaggerated, and the similarities suppressed, for polemical purposes.

Thucydides was one of the first to write something which we wish to identify as history: an account of the actions of people in the past, based on his interpretation of the available evidence. He sought to persuade his audience to accept his conclusions about events, but his account had to compete

with other kinds of stories, many of them far more prestigious and authoritative – for example, the works of Homer,
which were read not just as poems but as sources of knowledge and guidance and a foundation of the Greeks' sense of
identity. This may well account for the polemical way in
which Thucydides 'invents' history by attacking the credibility of his rivals, even Homer. Modern historians, in contrast,
operate from a position of power; it is widely accepted that
history has a monopoly on truth in accounts of the past (the
real problem comes from the fact that the past is simply felt
to be irrelevant, hence the prestige of 'present-centred' disciplines like economics and sociology). Nevertheless, both
modern and ancient historians employ the same methods to
establish the authority of *their* accounts, contrasting 'proper'
history (in other words, their sort of history) with other ways
of talking about past events.

Fiction

Thucydides first contrasted his work with that of the poets,
who also wrote about the deeds of men in the past. He didn't
accuse them of lying – and he was quite willing to make use
of Homer's work as a source for the early history of Greece
– but he did note that they tended to exaggerate the importance of their themes. In other words, they were prepared to
go beyond the evidence for the sake of entertaining their
audience. Other ancient writers echoed this opinion. The
philosopher Aristotle argued in his treatise on poetry that

historians relate actual events whereas poets relate the kind
of things that *might* occur (*Poetics* 1451b). Lucian claimed in
his essay on *How to Write History* that history and poetry have
different aims and rules: 'in the latter freedom is absolute and
there is one law, the judgement of the poet' (8). Modern
historians seek in a similar manner to distinguish their work
from that of the historical novelist, who draws on the same
evidence as they do to reconstruct the past.

'Poetry' comes from the Greek *poieo*, I make or do: it is
something which is made, produced by the imagination of
the poet. 'Fiction' comes from the Latin *fingo*, I shape, ar-
range, devise, represent, imagine. History is neither poetry
nor fiction: hence (so the contrast implies) it is not something
made or imagined by historians but a true representation of
the past. Historians do not invent things, they base their
conclusions on the evidence alone. The past is something
which is real, existing outside their accounts of it; historians
play no part in shaping or creating this past, they merely let
the facts speak for themselves. The purpose of the contrast
with fiction is clear, to privilege history as the only true
account of what really happened. Novels may be entertaining, they may even draw on the same evidence as the
historians do, but they are not history and so are not to be
believed.

We usually distinguish between history and fiction on the
basis of the form in which these different accounts of past
events are presented to us. From the title of the book, its
cover design and its location in the library or bookshop to

the style in which it is written, we receive a series of signals designed to identify it as a particular kind of account. We have learnt to recognise these signals, to associate one style of writing with history and another with fiction. We know that proper history rarely if ever includes passages of dialogue, and that novels rarely if ever have footnotes and bibliographies. Moreover, novelists are usually identified by their name alone, or perhaps also by a list of their previous works; historians normally make sure that their professional standing is prominently displayed on the back cover or the title page. Finally, only one sort of writing is likely to appear on essay bibliographies. On the basis of such clues we determine which accounts are to be read as authoritative and factual and which ones should be read just for entertainment.

Aristotle remarked that 'Herodotus' work could be put into verse and would be just as much history in verse as in prose' (*Poetics* 1451b). Few modern historians seem to be so confident about this; at any rate, they resolutely cling to the conventional style of historical writing, so that their works could never be confused in any way with fiction. At the same time they hold firmly to the view that the significant difference between history and fiction is not form but content. History, it is argued, is written in a particular style because this is the most appropriate way of presenting a reliable, factual account of the past. Fiction is not intended to provide a factual account, and so novelists can afford to indulge in literary flourishes. Once again, we return to our culture's basic assumption that history and fiction are entirely distinct and that history provides us with the only true account of what happened in the past. Upon closer examination, however, the boundary between the contents of historical and fictional accounts becomes rather more blurred and uncertain.

As far as subject matter is concerned, fiction almost invariably focuses on the actions and thoughts of individuals, while most (though not all) history is more concerned with abstractions such as 'society' or 'slavery'. However, novelists can't ignore the wider context within which their characters think and act; and historians can't ignore the fact that the history of an institution like ancient slavery is made up of countless individual histories, of slaves, slave-owners and commentators on slavery – even if there isn't enough evidence to say anything much about the lives of each of those individuals. Something similar can be said of the aims of these different kinds of writing: both seek to persuade their readers of the truth of their representation of past events, even if fiction places more emphasis on entertainment and history stresses its educational role.

The key difference between historians and historical novelists lies in their methodologies, the ways in which each uses the available evidence to produce an account of past events. Above all, it lies in the role generally allowed to the writer's imagination. The historian, it is said, should never go beyond the evidence, and must as a consequence present an incomplete, fragmentary account of the past if the evidence is incomplete and fragmentary. The novelist is at liberty to invent people, dialogue and even events if the story demands it. Indeed, many historical novels portray the involvement of entirely fictional characters in scrupulously researched historical events. In other words, some of the things that novelists tell us about the past may have no basis whatever in the evidence; we can trust that historians will always be able to offer some justification for everything they relate.

This distinction is certainly significant. It is also potentially misleading, in so far as it tends to imply that historians never use their imaginations in reconstructing the past. In fact, as I shall argue in the next chapter, imagination plays an indispensable role in the interpretation of evidence, helping the historian to make connections, fill in gaps and build up a wider picture of the period being studied. The methodological differences between history and fiction are therefore only a matter of degree: historians are not supposed to let their imaginations get too carried away. This is then reflected in the conventional forms of the different accounts: historians are expected to 'show their working', so to speak, to cite the evidence they have used in footnotes and bibliographies and to explain their reasoning, rather than just presenting their final conclusions as a seamless narrative. Finally, we should note the extent to which novelists are generally praised for their use of imagination whereas historians try to conceal their dependence on it.

The French historian Paul Veyne argued, paradoxically and provocatively, that history was 'un vrai roman', a true novel. The differences in form between history and fiction are a matter of convention and convenience, the differences in methodology are a matter of degree. History could be described as a type of fiction, governed by a particular set of generic conventions (including restrictions on the unbridled use of imagination). Indeed, before the nineteenth century history was seen as a genre of literature, a place for fine writing and rhetorical set-pieces as well as factual accuracy. The Roman rhetorician Quintilian regarded history as a kind of 'prose poem'; the reputations of historians like Sallust, Tacitus and Gibbon depend at least as heavily on their literary brilliance as on their reliability as reporters. Modern historians, however, emphasise the contrast between history and fiction in the hope of concealing the fictive nature of their own writings. The prestige of history would, it seems, be lessened if it was mistaken for fiction, something invented by the writer, rather than accepted as an objective account of the past in which the historian merely reports the facts.

Myth

Thucydides also contrasted his work with that of the logographers, compilers of stories about the past (among whom he probably included Herodotus). Such writers were more interested in pleasing their audience than in seeking out the truth; their authorities could not be checked, and the stories they collected were basically mythical and so not to be trusted. Thucydides stuck for the most part to contemporary history, which was not tainted with mythology, and based his

account only on trustworthy sources (his own experience and
the reports of eye-witnesses), which he subjected to critical
analysis. The invention of history by the Greeks is often
presented as the victory of *logos* over *muthos*, of a new form of
rational enquiry over the old myths.

'Myth' is, if anything, even more difficult to define than
'history' – though that does not lessen the force of the
contrast. We 'know' that a myth is a fabulous story, the sort
that begins 'Once upon a time ...', involving heroes and
monsters. History must therefore be a true story about the
real past. However, scholars hoping to understand the meaning and function of myths have attempted to devise more
precise definitions. The problem is that they disagree on
which stories are to be counted as 'proper' myths, depending
on their view of the function of myths in society. Thus,
Geoffrey Kirk wishes to distinguish between myths and
legends on the grounds that legends (such as King Arthur or
Robin Hood) are too historical, whereas others would happily class Arthur as a mythical figure *regardless* of whether he
existed or not.

The most helpful definition is that devised by Walter
Burkert: 'a myth is a traditional tale with secondary, partial
reference to something of collective importance'. A myth is
a story, told and retold but retaining the same basic form,
handed down from generation to generation; but a story with
some deeper significance, embodying the values of the com-
munity, forming part of people's sense of identity,
legitimising some practice or institution. Every culture has

such myths, and any story – including historical stories – may become a myth. The Greeks had stories about heroes, monsters, gods and Amazons (culture *versus* nature, the place of humans between beasts and gods); the English have the Spanish Armada, Trafalgar, Dunkirk and the Blitz (Britons as plucky and freedom-loving despite adversity); Americans have the Mayflower, Washington and the cherry tree, the frontier and Manifest Destiny.

History can become myth; myth can become history (see Thucydides' attempt to reconstruct the early history of Greece, 1.2-19, and more sophisticated modern attempts to reconstruct the mental world of the Greeks through their myths). How far is it possible to draw a clear line between them? Once again, the obvious but unhelpful answer is that we usually do it on the basis of form and context: we simply don't expect to find myths masquerading as history (as opposed to myths being the subject of historical enquiry). The idea that the history we are taught might in fact be a myth is very unsettling; yet this is precisely what is argued by Martin Bernal. He claims that European classicists have promoted a particular view of the development of Greece, despite all the evidence that contradicts it, because it confirms their feelings of superiority over other races. Bernal's argument that Greek culture was in fact derived from Egypt can be seen as an attempt to popularise an alternative, non-racist myth of the origins of European civilisation.

Myths are often, though not always, decontextualised, set in the past but not a very specific past: 'once upon a time', 'ancient times', 'the Middle Ages', 'the War'. History is firmly tied to a chronological structure, and so we can make statements about precisely when an event took place. More importantly, there is a clear contrast in the ways in which each kind of story is produced, the intentions of their creators and the expectations of their audience. Myths are not created by an individual but by the retelling of stories in different contexts – bedtime stories, public performances, visual representations – until they become part of the 'cultural heritage' of society. History is created by a historian, who examines stories from the past so as to assess their reliability, criticising and comparing them. Myth is about the telling of stories for pleasure, even if those stories also have a deeper meaning; history ostentatiously claims to be concerned with the truth of what happened, regardless of whether it makes a good story or has any deeper meaning.

Clearly there are grounds for making some distinction between myth and history in terms of their attitude to stories about the past: history is consciously critical, myth is not. However, this contrast should not be pushed too far; above all, it must not be interpreted as saying that history is automatically true and myth automatically false. Another misleading implication of the contrast is that, because myth is clearly bound up with the values and institutions of society, history is therefore in some way independent, neutral and objective.

In investigating past history, and in forming the conclusions

which I have formed, it must be admitted that one cannot
rely on every detail which has come down to us by way of
tradition. People are inclined to accept all stories of ancient
times in an uncritical way – even when these stories concern
their own native countries ....

Thucydides 1.20

Thucydides twice discussed the 'historical myth' of the Athenian tyrannicides (1.20 and 6.54-9). He pointed out that the
tyranny had actually been overthrown by the Spartans; that
Harmodius and Aristogeiton had killed the tyrant's brother,
not the tyrant himself, and only because they had panicked;
that the whole affair arose out of sexual jealousy and pique
rather than any higher motive, and that the death of Hippar-
chus actually led to greater oppression for the Athenians. All
of this was designed to undermine one of the charter-myths
of the Athenian democracy, which embodied the key ideal of
resistance to tyranny. This was an overtly political and sub-
versive act, but one which Thucydides could excuse by
claiming that he was really only interested in the facts, whatever they turned out to be.

Myths are regarded as stories told by the ignorant and
credulous masses: history is expert knowledge for the educated and intelligent, and is therefore clearly superior, at least
in the eyes of historians. The contrast between them is
significant, since history certainly aims at offering a more
critical account of the past. However, it also serves to conceal
the extent to which historians may themselves be dependent
upon myths or even involved in producing or justifying

them (think of Bernal's critique of the dominant nineteenth-century view of the Greeks). Myths are always bound up with the values and institutions of the society that produces them – but so too is history, however much historians may try to pretend otherwise.

Propaganda

Something similar can be said of the contrast between history and propaganda, or other sorts of 'official' history. Countless historians over the centuries have stressed the need for objectivity and freedom from partisanship in writing about the past. Thucydides talked of the partiality of some of his sources for one side or the other, implying that he was free from such bias. Sallust insisted that history should be free from hope, fear and partisanship; Tacitus vowed to avoid the twin pitfalls of flattery and invective. According to Lucian the historian should, among other things, be 'in his books a stranger and a man without a *polis*, independent, subject to no king, not reckoning what this or that man will think, but stating the facts' (41). Modern historians often mention with horror the re-writing of history at the command of authoritarian governments in Hitler's Germany and the old Soviet Union.

History should, according to this view, be an objective account of the facts, free from any external interference or influence. Whether this is actually possible, or even desirable, will be discussed at greater length later in this book, but on the whole the answer appears to be no. Historians cannot escape the fact that they have been formed by a particular set of external influences; a Russian ex-communist will see the world (and its past) in a rather different way from a Sikh, men and women will have different ideas about history, and so forth. Historians cannot prevent their personalities and opinions from 'distorting' their view of the past, unless they confine themselves to the most basic (and boring) discussions of the evidence. The contrast between 'proper' history and propaganda nevertheless serves to suggest that such detachment is possible: since history is not so blatantly biased, it must therefore be entirely neutral and bias-free, and hence more reliable.

This is quite clearly a rhetorical device, intended to persuade the reader to accept the historian's conclusions; this account is tainted by flattery, that one is clearly inspired by hatred, trust *me*. The Byzantine historian Procopius (sixth century AD) made this sort of claim both in his oleaginous and adulatory account of the emperor Justinian's wars and in his vicious and salacious *Secret History* of the same period. This has naturally disturbed later historians enormously: these accounts cannot both be true, so which one did the author really want us to believe? The *Secret History* is obviously unreliable, with its stories of the emperor's demonic powers and the empress's sexual exploits, but its mere existence calls into question Procopius' sincerity when he asked us to believe his more sober version of events in the *History of the Wars*. The only sensible conclusion seems to be that we cannot accept either account at face value. It is at least conceivable that this is the conclusion that Procopius intended us to draw. History is not a special, intrinsically unbiased account of the past to be contrasted with official propaganda or unbridled polemic; all such accounts are equally compromised, equally implicated in structures of power in society, competing with one another to persuade readers to accept their version of events.

Science

The vast majority of historians would agree, rightly or wrongly, that history is qualitatively different from myth, fiction and propaganda. There is far less agreement, at least in the English-speaking world, over whether or not history should be described as a science. Part of the problem is inevitably due to disagreement over the definition of science. The word derives from the Latin *scio*, I know. In many other languages, the words used to translate 'science' (*science, sapienza, wissenschaft*) cover 'knowledge' in general, and so happily incorporate history along with economics, biology and particle physics. The philosopher and historian R.G. Collingwood took this line in his definition of history:

> Every historian would agree, I think, that history is a kind of research or enquiry. What kind of enquiry it is I do not yet ask. The point is that generically it belongs to what we call the sciences; that is, the forms of thought whereby we ask questions and try to answer them.

In English, however, the word science is far more closely associated with the natural sciences – physics, chemistry, biology. A subject like economics is classified as 'social science' rather than just 'science'. Collingwood's definition of history as science tends to look like philosophical sleight-of-hand: Humpty Dumpty in Lewis Carroll's *Alice in Wonderland* making words mean what he wants them to mean. It ducks the real issue of how history does in fact relate to these familiar forms of knowledge.

It is easy enough to distinguish between history and the natural sciences on the basis of their institutional organisation (different faculties in the university) and the style of their writings. Traditionally, there was thought to be an obvious difference in their chosen subject matter, since scientists studied the natural world and historians studied people, but the boundaries have been confused in recent decades with the development of environmental history and ecology. The key argument has always been over the question of methodology. The standard view of science is that it proceeds by formulating hypotheses and then testing them, above all by the use of experiments. The scientist is a detached observer who uses objective systems of measurement; the scientist aims at discovering the laws which govern the physical world, and using these laws scientists can not only explain things which have happened but also make accurate predictions (for example, plotting the future course of a comet).

Some historians have concluded from this that, while history is clearly not identical to the natural sciences, it is

sufficiently similar to be classed as a science – and should
perhaps be made more like a science. History too proceeds
by formulating hypotheses and testing them against the evidence. Historians are not able to make use of experiments
(re-running the Fall of the Roman Empire under slightly
different conditions to see what difference it would make),
but then neither can certain branches of the natural sciences
like geology or cosmology. The historian is of course always
detached and objective, just like the scientist. Some writers
have indeed tried to uncover the laws which govern human
behaviour, but all historians make generalisations about the
way in which societies work. It is only in the field of prediction that history is an unqualified failure in comparison to
science.

Indeed, it could be argued that history is not scientific
enough. Its theories should be formulated and tested explicitly; historians should concentrate on the sorts of data that
can be measured objectively without recourse to subjective
evaluation, like price series or demographic records (hence
the branch of economic history known as Cliometrics); they
should strive to be ever more detached and 'scientific', even
adopting the terminology and style of scientific writing in
place of the woolly literary style in which most history is
written. The 'social sciences' like economics and sociology
have gone furthest in adopting scientific methods and style,
hoping to study society in exactly the same way as one might
study the structure of DNA or the atom. Historians have
tended to be consumers rather than producers of laws,

applying the insights of the social sciences to particular historical events rather than formulating propositions about human behaviour in general on the basis of their studies – but that is no reason why they should not change their practices, and contribute a historical perspective to the project of understanding the workings of society in scientific terms.

Other historians have reacted with horror to this approach to history, and to the idea that history has anything in common with the natural sciences. They emphasise the impossibility of doing historical experiments and the failure of historians to predict the future with any success. They stress the differences between the sorts of evidence used by geologists and cosmologists in reconstructing the past (products of natural processes like volcanoes and the Big Bang) and that used by historians (products of human activity, above all human thought). Above all, they reject the idea that there are laws of history (or of human society). Human beings, it is argued, are not predictable; their actions are not wholly determined by their own biology or by their society or environment, but they have some measure of free will. The scientific approach to history is anti-humanistic and fatally flawed – as seen in the failure of historians (and other social scientists) to predict the future, even though they claim to have uncovered the laws of human behaviour. History is an art, not a science, since the historian has to try to understand the actions and thoughts of other human beings rather than simply measure them – although of course it is a special kind of art, based on the rigorous interpretation of evidence and not at all dependent on the subjective judgement and imagination of the historian.

What is once more at stake in this debate is the prestige of history, the attempt to privilege the historical account (or a certain type of historical account) over other accounts of the past. Scientific language is an enormously successful and prestigious way of describing the world: the methods and products of natural science have enabled us over the last two centuries to dominate and change our environment and even our own selves. The scientific account of a phenomenon is, with a few exceptions (UFOs, perhaps), generally accepted in our society as true: scientists are seen as highly qualified experts who are neutral and disinterested – 'scientific', even – in their search for truth. If history can claim to be a science, it can buy into this image.

Science has been very successful in pushing alternative ways of describing the world – for example, the Judaeo-Christian story of the Creation – into marginal positions, but it has not succeeded in replacing them altogether. Plenty of arguments have been put forward against the scientific world-view, above all against the assumption that human beings can be understood wholly in terms of their genetic, psychological or social inheritance. Some historians have joined in this reaction, rejecting the scientific model of understanding human society as anti-humanistic and politically dubious (especially as Marxist accounts of the past were so keen to describe themselves as scientific). An absence of method and the repudiation of any kind of explicit theorising are hence considered to be virtues in writing history. Historians, it is said, can give a better account of the past, and even of the present, precisely because they have not fallen for the illusory certainties of scientific methodologies (unlike practitioners of competing subjects such as economics and sociology ...).

Whether different historians consider that history is a kind of science will clearly influence the way in which they write history: the sorts of questions they ask, the way in which they interpret evidence (whether or not they make use of theories from other disciplines, for example) and even their style of expression. The comparison between history and science can also tell us a great deal about attitudes to science in our society – though historians' reactions of adulation or suspicion seem to be equally based on an erroneous idea of what science is and how it works. It does not seem, however, that the comparison tells us very much at all about the nature of history. History and, say, physics are similar in some ways and very different in others; the same might be said of history and stamp-collecting, except that no historians have yet felt that they would enhance the prestige of their accounts by making such a comparison.

'Fringe' history

Although history has not succeeded in raising itself to the status of a full science (and many historians would resist such

a move even if it were possible), it has established itself over
the last two centuries as a respectable academic discipline
whose authority is guaranteed by its place in universities and
in the school curriculum. Despite the fact that many historians prefer to ignore theoretical issues or explicit discussions
of their methodology, history has come to be accepted as a
form of expert knowledge; only properly trained historians
have authority to say what the past was really like. History is
seen to offer a superior account. Fiction may be more evoca-
tive and entertaining, myth may be more comforting, but
history is (or rather, is taken to be) true.

Of course, historians disagree, at inordinate length, about
almost every aspect of the past, but this does not undermine
the authority of history as a whole. The real problem for
historians lies in deciding what should be allowed to call itself
history. What is to be done with books that claim to be based
on the critical analysis of evidence and are written in something resembling the accepted scholarly style, and yet are not
(at least in the eyes of historians) 'proper' history? Erich von
Däniken concluded from his researches that extraterrestrial
beings constructed the Pyramids and the statues on Easter
Island. Iman Wilkens analysed Homer's *Iliad* in great detail
and concluded that the Trojan War took place just outside
Cambridge. Books like these, on subjects such as the Holy
Grail, the Ark of the Covenant and other Great Unsolved
Mysteries of the World, are extremely popular, and far more
widely read than academic history; television programmes on
similar subjects reach millions.

A few historians and archaeologists respond, or are forced to respond, to this 'fringe history' by becoming professional sceptics, called in to play the voice of the establishment on television documentaries. The vast majority simply ignore the existence of such books; they are clearly not worth taking seriously. This is, I think, a very short-sighted attitude, for a number of reasons. In the first place, any historian must surely be concerned about the growing influence of this sort of history on popular perceptions of the past. Secondly, there is the more immediate problem that those reading such books include many students and potential students. I find myself at least once a year trying to mark a student assignment that is heavily dependent on sources which I consider to be quite plainly unreliable and bizarre. Students have to cope with the fact that their teachers may, apparently at random, turn out to be violently prejudiced against a particular book or author, with the resultant reduction in marks.

There is a case in favour of historians thinking more carefully about how they go about distinguishing 'fringe' or 'pseudo-' history from 'proper' history, and trying to teach this to their students. The critical evaluation of secondary texts is no less important a skill for the historian than the analysis of primary sources. This does, however, raise another problem. All too often, I suspect, certain books are rejected simply because their authors are not part of the historical establishment; history is defined as what historians accept as history. The works of writers like von Däniken and Wilkens are not published by respectable academic publishers (who ask established historians to vet manuscripts submitted to them); they are not reviewed in the respectable academic journals; they do not appear on the shelves of university libraries or on students' reading lists. Their authors are not offered academic posts – and the fact that they are not professional historians is often seen as the clinching argument that their views should not be taken seriously.

I do this myself all the time; my initial considerations in evaluating a book would certainly include its publisher, its cover blurb and its author's academic credentials, and these would certainly prejudice my reading of it. Up to a point, the approach works, if only as a guarantee of minimum standards; the work of someone who holds an academic post or is published by a reputable academic publisher has, at some time or another, been scrutinised by other ancient historians. Clearly, however, this is not a test of the reliability of the work but of the author's position in relation to the scholarly establishment. It is easy to see how the assumptions which allow the unthinking dismissal of von Däniken as a crank could easily be turned against other sorts of writings about the past. Indeed, they have often operated in this manner, justifying the rejection of Marxist history, feminist history, black history. Bernal's argument that the whole of ancient history has been contaminated by a racist myth can safely be ignored because Bernal is an expert in Chinese politics, not a trained classicist (as becomes all too clear when he moves on from historiography to writing about the ancient world).

There are some perfectly good reasons for treating the

views of someone like von Däniken with suspicion. He gets some evidence wrong (Easter Island did once have lots of trees, so it *was* possible to move the statues without the aid of spaceships), but, more importantly, his interpretation of the evidence is simply less convincing than other possible interpretations. It is not *necessary* to hypothesise alien visitors to explain how the Pyramids were constructed. I shall discuss the question of formulating and assessing interpretations in the next chapter. The key point is that von Däniken should not be dismissed because he is a former hotel manager rather than a trained historian, but because his argument is flawed and unconvincing. In the same way, a professor whose book has been published by Harvard University Press is not automatically right. All attempts at writing about the past need to be read equally critically.

What is history?

The past is important to people. As I shall argue at greater length in Chapter 4, their sense of personal, social and national identity is bound up with stories of past events, as is the authority and prestige of many institutions and customs. Different people and groups therefore seek to have their version of events accepted as the true account. Historians are inevitably part of this struggle to determine the meaning of the past. They seek to persuade their audience to accept the authority of history by claiming that their methods are uniquely unbiased and trustworthy, contrasting history with

myth, fiction and propaganda. Historians define and police
the boundaries of history so as to privilege their own version
of events over other kinds of account. It works entirely to
their advantage that we tend to take their idea of history for
granted, accepting that proper history is what historians do.

Our vague, woolly, common-sense idea of history is not
universally valid, though we tend to think of it as such, and
it is not actually very useful in determining what is and isn't
to be considered as history. However, a precise definition of
history may be equally misleading. On closer inspection, the
distinction between history and fiction or history and myth
is not clear-cut. If we try to define the boundary between
them, we tend to exaggerate the differences and ignore the
similarities. It is more productive – though less effective for
polemical purposes – simply to explore different aspects of
the relations between history and other accounts of the past.
There are important differences between history and novels,
for example, but that should not completely obscure everything that they have in common as narrative prose accounts,
the products (at least in part) of the imaginations of their
authors.

I have done my best in this chapter to avoid describing
history as a subject, a discipline, a kind of enquiry, a literary
genre or anything except 'a way of talking about the past'. A
more specific description would, I think, beg too many
questions and obscure too much of what history might be. If
we think of history as a subject or a discipline, emphasising
its place in the educational system – which is, after all, where

most of us first encounter it — we will be too inclined to discuss history only in terms of what professional historians do or claim to be doing. If we describe it as a kind of enquiry or a form of knowledge, we will tend to concentrate on historical methodology to the exclusion of all else (the style of historical writing, the institutional framework, the politics of historical interpretation and so forth). We hardly dare treat history as if it were no more than a particular genre of literature, ignoring its claims to be able to tell a true story about the past.

I find it most helpful to think of history as a particular way of talking — and writing and thinking — about the past. Alternatively, we might use the term 'discourse', understood as a network of conventions, knowledge and practices that together constitute 'history'. Such a loose definition encompasses all the different elements that constitute history as we understand it: its methodology and its literary style, its familiar institutional framework and the various forms of history found outside the educational establishment. This will nevertheless seem quite inadmissible to many historians: surely I am confusing what is essential to history (methodology) with what is secondary (style, institutional structures)? Well, as I said at the beginning of this chapter, there is no such thing as a neutral, unproblematic definition of history; all definitions are working to someone's advantage (in this case, mine, because I want to talk about all these things) at someone else's expense.

History is a form of discourse about the past. It is distin-

guished from other discourses about the past by its emphasis
on the critical analysis and interpretation of the surviving
traces of the past, though (as we shall see in the next chapter)
historians disagree violently over how they should go about
making use of evidence. History is conventionally presented
in the form of a prose narrative, governed by various (culturally specific) unwritten rules and expectations about what a
historical narrative should look like. In the late twentieth
century, we most commonly encounter history in particular
institutional contexts, in schools and universities, which play
an important part in determining the ways in which history is
understood and practised.

History is not myth; but that does not mean that it is
automatically true. History is not fiction; but that does not
mean that the historian's imagination plays no part in the
reconstruction of the past. History is not propaganda; but
that does not mean that it is therefore invariably neutral and
objective. The boundaries between these different discourses
are never clear-cut, and it is equally possible to argue that
history is a kind of fiction (although governed by certain
generic conventions), and a kind of myth (a story that helps
us make sense of the world), and a kind of propaganda (for
the historian's personal point of view, if nothing else). We
know history when we see it: a particular way of telling a story
about the past, which claims to offer a trustworthy account
of past events.

CHAPTER 2

The Use and Abuse of Sources

Sources

History is a particular way of telling a story about the past, which claims to offer a trustworthy account of events. How do we go about telling this kind of story? Since the past is no longer with us, we cannot base our account of it on direct observation. What we have to base it on instead are the traces of the past that have survived into the present. Past actions or events had consequences that we can observe today, and it is through the study of these 'fossils' that we can recover some idea of what once happened. For example, we can talk about the eruption of Mount Vesuvius in AD 79 because its impact on the surrounding countryside is still visible (most obviously at the sites of Pompeii and Herculaneum), and because people at the time wrote accounts of the eruption which have survived to the present day. Such traces of the past are generally referred to as 'sources' or 'evidence'. Traditionally, ancient historians have been most concerned with the written sources that have survived from antiquity, but the term 'source' should be taken to cover absolutely everything that bears the trace of the past and so may be used to produce a historical account.

The claim that history can offer a more trustworthy account of the past than other kinds of discourse is based primarily on the way in which historians make use of these sources. History, unlike myth or fiction, is concerned above all else with trying to recover the truth of 'how it really was': the *reality* of the past rather than just someone's impression of it. This may not actually be possible, as we shall see, but it is still the main aim of most historical writing. History, therefore, unlike myth, makes use of the whole range of sources relating to past events, comparing and contrasting them, and it treats these sources critically. History, unlike fiction, not only is based on the sources but also accepts the limits that they set on our knowledge. The historian's imagination is not supposed to wander too far in filling in the inevitable gaps in the sources or in producing interpretations of the significance and meaning of past events; the historian must sometimes admit to ignorance, if the sources for the subject in question are inadequate.

For many historians, the critical analysis of the sources *is* history; everything else (the form in which they present their conclusions, the social and institutional framework within which they work) is entirely incidental. History books often begin with discussions of the 'problems' of the sources, either their scarcity or their fragmentary nature, or some other feature which makes it difficult to use the sources in question as a basis for an historical account (for example, if a particular ancient author is felt to be unreliable). Disputes between historians are invariably concerned with the interpretation of the sources (it is not generally considered acceptable to criticise someone for writing a boring book, only for writing an unconvincing one). Students are constantly reminded of the need to pay attention to the sources and to refer to them in essays; they are given courses on 'Use of Sources', and advised to make use of sourcebooks, collections of extracts from ancient texts, where these are available for particular topics.

The sources are clearly important. What is not always so clear is what you are supposed to *do* with them. I hope I am not insulting too many people by suggesting that many students quote bits of ancient texts in their essays and assignments simply because they've been told to, not because they've actually developed their own interpretation of the past from reading the sources. The quotations are used to illustrate someone else's argument, taken from the secondary literature, not to support their own views. Since this practice is rewarded, while those who don't mention the sources at all are usually penalised (however well argued their work may be), it's quite understandable that students should respond in this way to their teachers' advice. In practice, they are not learning how to do history so much as how to write history essays, but they are generally given no other indication of how to proceed. In this chapter I shall discuss various issues relating to the ways in which historical sources *should* be used. There are two questions that we particularly need to consider. First, how do historians go about producing their interpretations of past events from the surviving traces of the past? Secondly, how far can we believe that their interpretations offer us a trustworthy picture of the past?

Facts

Historians talk a lot about facts. It has occasionally been argued that the sole purpose of history is to 'get the facts right', simply to produce an accurate account of what happened in the past. Most historians try to do more than this, aiming not only to establish what happened but also to explain why it happened and what the consequences were – in other words, to interpret the facts – but they would still stress the importance of facts in writing history. Facts are the foundations on which historians base their accounts, they are the building blocks with which they construct their arguments and reinforce and support their theories. Alternatively, facts are seen as witnesses to past events: some historians argue that the facts should be allowed to 'speak for themselves', others believe that they will get to the truth of what happened by asking them the right questions. The facts tell us, or may be forced to tell us, about the past: they suggest or imply that something is the case, they bear witness, they agree with or contradict one another.

The word 'fact' comes from the Latin *facio*, I make or do; a fact is something that was done, which happened. As a matter of fact, that's a fact, in fact: 'fact' quickly comes to mean something that is true and real. It is certainly a nice, solid word: how reassuring for the reader that the historical account is factual, not fiction or mere opinion. Further, the facts are talked about as though they have an independent existence outside the historical account – either as witnesses or as a pile of bricks, depending on your choice of metaphor. The task of the historian is to uncover these pre-existing facts, and then to interpret them. Interpretation is always subjective and personal, and so potentially unreliable or biased, but the facts are real. The more firmly a historian's interpretation is grounded in the 'reality' of the facts, the more it can be trusted to provide a solid, well-founded, water-tight reconstruction of 'how it really was' in the past. Or so historians hope to persuade their readers.

This picture of the way in which historians do history – first solid facts, then interpretation based on these facts – is misleading. Facts are not tangible objects or independent entities. A fact is a verbal statement, an idea, with no empirical existence outside people's minds. I can attempt to demonstrate to you that something is a fact by producing enough evidence, but I cannot actually give you a fact to touch. Facts are established (another building metaphor?) not through direct sensory experience but through discourse, according to a particular set of rules about how truth is to be determined. Hence it is not possible to separate 'objective' facts from 'subjective' interpretation: facts are established *through* acts of interpretation. The job of the historian is not simply to uncover and interpret a pre-existing set of facts. It is to determine, through the interpretation of the sources, what things are to be given the status of facts and hence used as the basis for a historical account.

The idea that facts are products of the human mind seems wrong to us. Facts are not invented or created, they are discovered, uncovered, revealed; facts simply *are*. Nevertheless, it is easy to think of examples showing how 'the facts', what people have believed to be true, have changed over time, as the criteria for determining whether something is true or not have changed. It is an incontrovertible fact that the earth orbits the sun – except that, during the Middle Ages, it was an incontrovertible fact that the sun orbits the earth. This is not to say that the earth did not start orbiting the sun until the sixteenth century. Rather, the idea of a heliocentric solar system became a 'fact', a generally accepted truth, only then, and only as a result of lengthy debate about the correct way of interpreting the available evidence. A fact is an interpretation that is so widely accepted that it can be taken for granted – until it is challenged, as happened eventually with the 'fact' that the earth was at the centre of the universe. A more problematic example is the theory of evolution; accepted without question as a fact by most of us, but rejected as atheistic propaganda by those who use different criteria (e.g. compatibility with the Bible) for determining truth.

Anyone opening a history book is confronted with a wide range of facts: that is, statements that are assumed to be true and which therefore form the basis of the historian's account. Some of these facts will be entirely uncontentious, since the evidence in favour of their being true is overwhelming and because alternative interpretations of this evidence seem so far-fetched. Only the most manic conspiracy theorist would question the fact that the Battle of Hastings took place in 1066, or that a man landed on the moon in 1969, or that the Holocaust took place. In other cases, the facts are a matter of dispute, because the evidence can be interpreted plausibly in a number of different ways. The problem for the reader lies in deciding which facts can be taken for granted and which should be accepted only after careful consideration of the available sources. It is a fact that Caesar crossed the Rubicon and invaded Italy in 49 BC; going back to the sources in an attempt to prove or disprove this would be as much a waste of time as reinventing the wheel. It is an equally indisputable fact that Caesar *says* in his account that he was compelled to do this for fear of what his enemies might do otherwise. It is a matter of opinion and argument whether it is a fact that this was the real reason for his action – especially as other, less charitable, accounts of his motives have also survived. The statement 'Caesar crossed the Rubicon for fear of his enemies' is a fact only if you accept one interpretation of the sources (taking Caesar at his word) rather than another (well, he would say that, wouldn't he?).

Another example: 'The massive influx of slaves into Italy, especially after the final defeat of Carthage in 146 BC, brought about the catastrophic decline of the Italian peasantry'. It's the sort of sentence that crops up in exam papers

with the word 'Discuss' added at the end, and the key to
answering such questions is to identify which of the 'facts' it
offers need to be subjected to careful criticism. It is certainly
a fact that Carthage was finally defeated by the Romans in
146. It is also a fact that large numbers of slaves were
imported into Italy during the second and first centuries BC
(though some historians have recently started to wonder
quite how 'massive' this influx was: something which has
been a generally accepted fact for decades or centuries can
easily become a matter of dispute, or even abandoned altogether. In other words, don't rely too heavily on older
textbooks.). The final part of the statement is the crux of the
matter. It is a fact that some Roman writers describe the crisis
of the peasantry and blame it on the import of slaves, but
plenty of historians have argued that the sources should not
be taken literally and that there was in fact no such decline.
The student is being asked to review the evidence and the
way in which earlier historians have interpreted it to establish
whether it is a fact that the peasantry declined, and, if so,
whether it is a fact that this decline was caused by the influx
of slaves.

A fact is an interpretation that is so widely accepted that it
can be taken for granted – until it is challenged. One lesson
you might draw from this is that the historian needs to be
constantly vigilant and sceptical, taking nothing for granted
– although in practice, especially if you have only a week to
write the next piece of work, you do have to take quite a lot
on trust. Another lesson is that this is simply what history is

like: it is not built on the solid foundations of independent, pre-existing facts, but on the shifting , subjective sands of argument and interpretation.

Selection

The human brain is innately selective. From the vast array of sensory data that it receives every second, it isolates information that seems to be significant. Think of the way in which you can filter out certain sounds, like the ticking of a clock or the noise of traffic, if you're concentrating on what someone's saying. This is the only way of making sense of everything we see and hear and avoiding information overload. Similarly, we don't remember every detail of everything that happened to us in the past, only what is felt to be important or which relates to something important: I doubt if you can remember what you ate on the evening of 21 March 1997, unless it was your birthday or some other significant event. Finally, if we are describing an incident to someone, we don't tell them absolutely everything (not if we want to keep their attention, anyway). We select what seem to be the most important points, the things we think they most need to know to understand what we're saying.

The relevance of all of this for ancient history is obvious when we consider how our written sources were produced. None of them offers a complete account; and the information they provide is not a random selection from all the things they might have told us, but a selection based on the writer's

idea of what was important. Inevitably, the selection will be
subjective and personal, determined by the writer's own
interpretation of what happened – or the interpretation that
he wants to persuade us to accept. Think of the different
accounts that might be given of, say, the battle of Salamis.
The Greek generals would show how they judged their
tactics to perfection (though they might differ in the importance they ascribed to the actions of Themistocles). The
Persian generals would explain how adverse conditions and
Greek trickery foiled their otherwise foolproof plan of battle;
a Persian sea-captain would argue that he fought valiantly but
was let down by the mistakes of his superiors, and so forth.
None of these accounts need involve any invention or distortion; they simply present the facts as their authors saw
them, or the facts which fit their understanding of what
happened.

Unfortunately, we (unlike Thucydides, say) are hardly ever
in a position to compare different eye-witness accounts of an
incident in the past, in the hope of piecing together what
really happened. Instead we have to rely on the accounts
given by contemporary historians and other writers, who
have (supposedly) drawn on the accounts of different witnesses: in other words, made their own selection of
significant facts from selective accounts, according to their
own understanding of what happened. Both a Greek and a
Persian historian might claim to offer an overall picture of
the action at Salamis, and their accounts would presumably
have some incidents in common, but the overall interpreta-

tion and the facts they chose to report would be very different. Unfortunately, it remains true that the victors usually get to write the history; we don't have the Persian version to set against that of Herodotus.

Further, writers selected facts according to their conception of the subject and the expectations of their audience; Greek and Roman historians tell us a lot about war and politics, and next to nothing about society or economy, because they considered that the role of history was to record 'great deeds'. They included things that they thought might interest their audience, or which might help to make a moral or a political point. More frequently, they omitted things that they knew their readers knew already. Romans didn't need to be told how Roman politics worked, so Roman comments on the subject tend to be rather oblique; we get far more information – though not necessarily reliable information – from Polybius, who was a Greek writing about the Romans for a Greek audience. In recent decades, historians have responded to this problem by approaching the sources in a different way; they read between the lines, trying to see what the sources reveal about the unconscious assumptions of the writers and their audience, rather than reading them in the way that their authors intended. This doesn't of course, solve the problem of gaps and omissions in the sources; it simply circumvents it, by asking a different set of questions.

None of this should be surprising; we can see how newspaper accounts of an event differ widely in the facts they choose to report or to emphasise, even when the writers are not attempting to put a particular slant on the story, and are writing news reports rather than an editorial. It must, however, affect the way in which we view the written sources. Most of our 'facts' about the ancient world are of the order 'Polybius says that the Romans did such-and-such'. It is an act of interpretation, based on what we know both of the Romans and of Polybius, to decide whether what he says is true and the Romans *did* do such-and-such (of course, the fact that Polybius *thinks* the Romans did it may still be significant in a different context; discussing Greek views of the Roman Empire, for example). We must always remember that the facts which Polybius provides are a selection, made both unconsciously (according to his own assumptions and preconceptions) and consciously (according to his artistic purposes) from all the things he *might* have told us. We never receive the full story, only Polybius' version of it.

Not everything that happened in the ancient world was recorded. Furthermore, it is obvious that not all the books ever written in antiquity have survived to the present; nor have all the buildings, inscriptions, artefacts and other things that we use as sources. *Tempus edax rerum*: time the devourer of things (Ovid); what has survived is a selection, and it seems too much to hope that it is a completely random selection. Memories last no longer than a human life, unless they can be passed on to a new generation – and only some memories will be handed down in this way, and, as in the game of Chinese Whispers, there is always the risk of distortion and omission in retelling the tale. If the words are written

down, they can last longer; but paper, parchment and
papyrus all decay in the end (unless they are preserved in
exceptional conditions, like the papyrus fragments found
buried in the desert or wrapped around mummies). For a
book to survive it must be preserved and copied, and not all
books received that privilege.

Of course, it's misleading to talk here of 'books'; for most
of antiquity, literature was written on and read from papyrus
rolls. When the codex, which is the direct ancestor of the
modern book, was adopted between the second and fourth
centuries AD, the works of writers who were popular at the
time were copied out from the rolls. The works of other
writers were not copied, and so had a far lower chance of
survival. From the fifth century onwards, the copying of
manuscripts lay in the hands of monks, who naturally preferred some books to others (for example, they preserved the
philosophy of Plato, which was felt to be compatible with
Christianity, but not that of Aristotle – which was, however,
preserved by the Arabs). Many pagan works survived this
period only because their pages were reused; the writing was
erased so that a Christian work could be copied out on top,
but enough of a trace was left for later scholars to recover the
original text. The works of writers like Cicero, Livy, the elder
and younger Pliny, Vergil and Ovid were all preserved in such
'palimpsests'. Many other works must have been lost. In part,
this process of selection was accidental; in part, it was a
matter of the deliberate choice of which texts should be
copied.

Non-literary evidence went through a similar process of selection and destruction. Above all, this depended on the perishability of the material. Stone and pottery survive the passage of time well (although stone blocks may be reused in later buildings). Wood and cloth decay rapidly except in exceptional conditions (hot and dry, like the Egyptian desert, or cold and wet, like bogs). Metals such as gold or iron would survive well were it not for the fact that they are valuable and so tended to be melted down and reused. We therefore have lots of evidence for ancient trade in wine and oil, which were transported in pottery amphorae, and virtually nothing for the far more important grain trade, since corn was carried in cloth sacks. Some pagan temples survived because they were converted into Christian churches; buildings for which no use could be found were demolished and the stones reused. The material evidence which is now available to us has also been selected by the activities of archaeologists: where they choose to dig and what sorts of things they're looking for. Nineteenth-century archaeologists were interested primarily in art objects and other prestigious finds, and so had no interest in excavating lower-class buildings or in preserving bits of bone, carbonised seeds and other things that might tell us something about 'everyday life' in antiquity. Modern archaeologists conducting field surveys of a region have to make decisions about the intensity of the survey, which affect the amount and the nature of the evidence likely to be collected.

This process of selection over time, both random and

deliberate, affecting both literary and material evidence, is often seen as the greatest problem for anyone attempting to do ancient history. There are so many gaps in our sources, and the evidence that has survived is rarely sufficient to prove or disprove a point beyond reasonable doubt. Above all, there is the problem of arguments from silence: is absence of evidence to be considered evidence of absence? If we demand incontrovertible proof for everything, we shall be unable to say anything much about ancient history (let alone anything interesting). How far can we go in arguing instead that relevant evidence might once have existed but wasn't the sort of thing likely to have survived the process of selection? How far can we go, indeed, in arguing that the evidence may have been deliberately suppressed?

A classic example is the question of whether Roman senators were ever involved in large-scale commerce. We know that some writers (most notably Cicero) claimed that it would be demeaning for a senator to be involved in trade; we don't have any direct evidence that senators ever were involved. For some, this is sufficient proof that Cicero spoke the truth; others argue that, since it was seen to be demeaning, any senator who was involved in trade would be careful to conceal this fact, so we wouldn't expect to *find* any evidence. In extreme cases, this verges on the *X-Files* Theory of History: the truth is out there, but is being systematically covered up. However, given the state of the sources, all ancient historians have to accept that the evidence we have is only a selection, and not an entirely random selection, of

all the books ever written and all the artefacts ever produced.
We must always take account of the possibility that the vital
piece of evidence that would change our whole interpretation
may have been accidentally lost or deliberately discarded at
any time in the last two millennia.

Ancient historians sometimes give the impression that, if
only the sources were more plentiful and less fragmentary,
we could move towards a properly objective account of 'how
it really was' in the past. The more we know, it is suggested,
the better we will understand. This idea rests on the assumption that each piece of evidence has a single message, a
particular meaning that fits into our total understanding of
antiquity like a piece of a jigsaw. On the contrary, a fact has
no innate meaning; it acquires meaning only when it is put
together in a particular way with other facts. The more
evidence there is – for example, if a Persian account of
Salamis had survived, or clear evidence of a Roman senator
being involved in trade – the more obvious it becomes that
modern historians, too, make their selection from the available facts and give priority to ones which are felt to be
important in the context of their overall interpretation of
events. Suppose that evidence was found which showed
beyond doubt that a certain Roman senator was involved in
commerce. A historian might still believe that the weight of
evidence is against the idea that this happened regularly, and
so dismiss a single exception as irrelevant; another might see
this as the clinching proof that the old theory is flawed. In
producing our account of Salamis we would still have to

select which statements in each, equally partial, account should be accepted as fact. This would depend on our opinion of the reliability of the respective writers and our conception of the battle itself; there is no reason why another historian might not interpret the accounts in a different way. The 'problem' for ancient history is not so much the lack of evidence as the question of how to interpret the evidence we have, and how to decide between different interpretations of the same evidence.

Interpretation (1)

Four facts about the ancient world:

(i)   C. Vibius Postumus of Larinum was suffect consul in AD 5.
(ii)   The Latin word for 'money' is *pecunia*.
(iii)   The Latin word for a herd of cows is *pecus*.
(iv)   Over 24,000 Dressel 1 amphorae have been excavated from the bed of the River Saône in France.

The most reasonable response to any of these statements is, I think, 'So what?' All of these facts can reasonably be considered as true, and none of them tells us anything much; facts quite clearly do not speak for themselves. The historian's task is not simply to 'get the facts right'; rather, it is to interpret the facts, to bring out their possible meaning and significance, to show how they relate to other facts and how these facts may be brought together to produce an account of the past. An equally vital skill – perhaps even more important for ancient history students – is that of evaluating the interpretations of other historians, both their interpretations of individual facts and the ways in which they combine those facts to produce wider interpretations of the past.

I want to approach this topic by thinking about how we might interpret the four facts given above. How do we determine what they mean, and how they can be fitted into a wider picture? Briefly, I suggest that that interpretation is about making connections and evaluating their plausibility and usefulness; we make sense of individual facts by relating them to their 'context', which is itself derived from the interpretation of lots of other facts. I hope that what I mean will become clearer as we look at these examples in detail. Before we begin, however, I want to return for a moment to the question of how historians talk about their facts. Many historians – myself included – tend to treat facts as if they are witnesses to past events; they are said to speak, reveal, confirm and so forth. The implication of this metaphor is that every fact has a true story to tell, which the historian must elicit through careful listening or skilful interrogation. I think this is misleading, another rhetorical trick by which we historians try to present our interpretations of the past as *really there* in the facts, uniquely objective and reliable. On the contrary, as I hope to demonstrate, facts have no intrinsic meaning waiting to be revealed by historians; they are given meaning by the historians who interpret them – and different, but equally plausible, interpretations are always possible.

If we need a metaphor at all, I prefer to think of facts as bricks, which can be used to build anything from a cathedral to a pigsty – or simply thrown through somebody's window.

Before we can begin to interpret the facts, we have to determine what are to be considered as facts – which, as I've already suggested, we do through the interpretation of the sources. To take the first example: we have two inscriptions which have survived from the Roman period, one listing the names of the consuls for each year (including, for AD 5, C. Vibius Postumus as suffect consul) and the other, found on the site of Larinum and so assumed to be from that town, commemorating C. Vibius Postumus, who is described there as consul. Since these were official inscriptions, it seems reasonable to accept what they say as true; it also seems reasonable to assume that they are both referring to the same man. We haven't proved that this consul actually came from Larinum, only that he received an honorific inscription there. We have to decide, based in part on what we know of practices elsewhere in Italy and in part on our own intuition, whether it is more likely that the municipal authorities would honour a native of the town rather than an outsider.

In other words, we establish that our first fact is true (or at any rate plausible) by making a connection between two different sources and interpreting them in the light of other information, about epigraphic practices in Italy. We might also quote part of one of Cicero's speeches, where he states that a Sextus Vibius was one of those who were proscribed in Larinum by a man called Oppianicus during the dictator-

ship of Sulla. If our interpretation of the text (considered in
the context of what we know about Cicero, and the tradition
of Roman oratory, and the history of the period) persuades
us to accept this story as factual, and if we think it is likely
that this Sextus Vibius was a relation rather than a complete
stranger (depending on whether we think 'Vibius' was a
common name), then this supports the theory that our C.
Vibius Postumus also came from Larinum. Note that the
sources themselves can't tell us whether we can trust them,
or whether the connections we make are plausible. That
comes down to our personal judgement, as we try out different interpretations to see how well they fit the available
evidence.

   In fact, the process of interpretation starts even earlier
than this; we have to determine what the sources are actually
saying before we can start to evaluate the truth of what they
say. The Larinum inscription reads as follows: 'C·VIBIO·C·F· /
·POSTUMO· / ·PR·PRO·COS· / ·MUNICIPES·ET· / ·INCOLAE·'
(note that with some inscriptions – this one was quite legible
when it was first studied – even identifying the letters may
involve guesswork and interpretation). How do we go about
making sense of this? There is no label on the first two
groups of letters to *say* that they represent someone's name.
We recognise them as such by looking at them in the context
of our knowledge of the Latin language and of the conventions of Roman inscriptions. This tells us that Roman
inscriptions almost always have a name near the beginning,
either of the person who put up the inscription or of the

principal subject; that Romans normally had three names, of
which the first was always abbreviated in inscriptions; that
they generally included their father's name in abbreviation;
that the 'o' ending suggests that this may be a second declen-
sion noun in the dative or ablative singular. Once we've made
all these connections, we can determine that this is an inscription dedicated *to* (dative case) Caius Vibius Postumus, son of
Caius. We make sense of the rest of the inscription by relating
it to other inscriptions (which gives us some idea of what the
abbreviations PR and COS might stand for) and to the whole
Latin language (which suggests how we might translate a
word like 'municipes').

Every such translation, every move between one language
and another, is an act of interpretation; we try to make a
plausible connection between words in different languages.
This becomes clear if we look at the second and third facts
that I offered. The Latin *pecus* means *pecus*, no more. It is our
interpretation that *pecus* meant roughly the same to the Romans as 'herd' does to us; it may be *equivalent* to 'herd', but it
is certainly not the same. 'Herd' is the best translation we can
offer, but no translation is ever perfect; we always run the risk
of missing certain nuances that a word has in the original
language, and of introducing our own anachronistic understanding of the word in English. *Pecunia* offers a good
example of this. There is good reason to believe that the
Roman idea of money was quite different from our own —
they had coins whose value was related to the precious metal
content, we have token money, paper money and credit

cards. *Of course* our understanding of what 'money' means is very different from what the Romans understood by *pecunia* – but this is something that is not acknowledged if the word is simply translated as 'money'.

Another example: the Greek word πολις, *polis*, can be translated as 'city', or 'state', or 'city state'. Each of these translations is potentially misleading, failing to cover the whole significance of the word for the Greeks; there is no wholly adequate equivalent for *polis* in English. In recognition of this, many modern history books now leave the word transliterated, in italics, rather than trying to translate it. The word is highlighted, marked off; we are warned that the only adequate translation of the word *polis* would have to be at least a paragraph long in order to convey its full meaning. Other key terms – *ager publicus*, for example, or *plebs* – are often treated in the same way. In translating the Larinum inscription, I kept the term 'consul' rather than trying to find an English equivalent like 'chief magistrate' or 'president' – although that leaves the problem that 'consul' also has an English meaning, as in 'the American consul in Madrid'. In theory, however, *every* Greek or Latin word should be left in the original to warn us that something may be lost in translation. In practice, translation is unavoidable, but it is always approximate at best; a matter of interpretation, of trying to make a plausible connection between words in different languages.

In order to make sense of our sources and to decide what are to be considered facts, we need to interpret them, to set them in some sort of context. The same is true of material evidence; the classification of amphorae, or any other arte-facts, also involves an act of interpretation. On the basis of his study of the remains of thousands of Roman amphorae, a man called Dressel decided that they could be sorted into a number of different types on the basis of their shape, and that at least some of these types could be associated with a particular date and/or a particular place of origin. Later scholars have modified these categories (Dressel's Types 2, 3 and 4 are now treated as a single type, Dressel 2-4), but the principle remains the same. Archaeologists devote consider-able time and effort to identifying fragments of amphorae as belonging to a particular type, and on this basis draw conclu-sions about their dating and provenance. This is the only way in which such material can usefully be understood and used as evidence; fragments of pottery certainly don't speak for themselves. Likewise for coins, bones, remains of buildings and all other material evidence; archaeologists use their judgement to classify such objects according to the resem-blance to other objects, and then draw conclusions on the basis of this classification.

The story so far: we establish that certain things are facts through a process of interpretation, making sense of an inscription or a literary text or a fragment of amphora by relating it to everything else we know (above all, by relating it to other inscriptions, other texts, other amphorae). The procedure is the same when we try to make sense of these facts and give them meaning; we relate them to other facts, looking at them in the context of other things we know. The important thing to remember is that there is not a single correct way of doing this; any fact can be related to any other fact or considered in any context, and its meaning will change accordingly. Some connections are simply more obvious than others. To take our first example, the consulship of C. Vibius Postumus, we need first of all to relate this fact to what we know of the Roman political system so as to understand what a suffect consul was; we must also have recourse to our knowledge of the geography of Roman Italy to learn more about Larinum. Thereafter, we have a free choice, depending on what sort of account of the past we wish to produce.

We could relate this fact to the other things we know about C. Vibius Postumus (not much, actually), so as to write his biography. We could add it to everything else we know about Larinum, so as to write a history of the town. The historian Ronald Syme compared Vibius with other men who held the consulship around this time, and concluded that they were all members of an 'Augustan party' drawing its strength from provincial Italy. The fact of C. Vibius Postumus' consulship will have a different significance in each of these accounts: it is the culmination of a successful career in the Roman Senate, *and* it is a sign of how Larinum maintained its links with the centres of power in Rome, *and* it is (arguably, at least) one more piece of evidence of the way that Augustus established control over the Roman state.

We can make sense of the other facts in the same way. It

is a straightforward act of interpretation to decide that there is some connection between *pecus* and *pecunia*. There is nothing in the two words to say that they *must* be connected, but their obvious similarity makes the idea plausible; moreover, at least one Roman author made the same connection. We can then argue that this shows that the Romans' ancestors lived in a pastoral society in which true wealth lay in the ownership of cattle. This hypothesis can be supported by reference to other information about early Roman society, and also to what we know about other primitive societies, many of which also measured wealth in terms of cattle. Alternatively, we could relate this bit of etymology to the way in which the Romans of the Augustan period talked about the past; they imagined a society without money, in contrast to their own, and pointed out the similarity of the two words as evidence of this. Once again, the fact is not limited to a single meaning; it can mean different things in different contexts. We don't get anywhere by just looking at the fact, waiting for it to reveal its true significance; we give it meaning by making connections, building up interpretations, fitting the fact into our accounts.

Is there any limit to the connections we can make? In theory, I think, no; or rather, the limits are practical ones, based on the plausibility and usefulness of the connections. Some will clearly be more obvious than others; relating an official inscription to the Roman political system, for example, or relating amphorae to trade networks. Still, precisely because they are obvious, such connections are rarely very interesting. They are certainly necessary as a first step in making sense of a fact – we couldn't interpret the Larinum inscription without setting it in the context of Roman politics – but they don't advance our understanding of the past to any significant extent. The real task of the historian is to go beyond the obvious, to suggest connections between different facts that change the way we think about the past. This is what Syme did with C. Vibius Postumus; in his account, this man's consulship was shown to be more significant than other historians had suspected. Likewise, the *pecus-pecunia* connection becomes interesting only when we relate it to other evidence, about the nature of pastoral societies or the way that the Romans thought about money.

Of course, not everyone has found Syme's attempts to link C. Vibius Postumus to other Italian notables entirely convincing; the theory doesn't contradict any of the surviving sources, but it does require you to accept the hypothesis of an 'Augustan party' for which there is no direct evidence. Interesting connections are always more tenuous and uncertain than the obvious ones, and we shouldn't reject them out of hand simply because of that. At the same time, however, we can never take it for granted that there is a connection between two facts, simply because a historian claims there is. We have to judge for ourselves how convincing their interpretation seems to be; how well it fits the facts, how much we are asked to accept on trust. In putting forward our own interpretations, we have to make them as convincing as possible; offering plenty of indirect evidence, explaining away evidence that seems to contradict our argument and so forth.

For example, suppose that we want to argue that Vibius was involved in the wine trade, something for which there is no evidence. We know that wine from Larinum was sold in Rome; we know that, as a senator, Vibius must have been a major landowner; surely he would have produced some wine on his estates, and sold it to raise money to fund his political activities? The evidence that contradicts this argument, Cicero's statement that it was demeaning for a senator to be involved in trade, can be explained away as a rhetorical gesture, an out-dated ideal rather than a picture of reality. In fact I don't think we are in any position to say whether or not Vibius ever produced or sold wine, but I hope this illustrates the sorts of arguments we need to put forward to justify our interpretations if there is no direct evidence either for or against them.

So: the connections we make between different facts should be plausible – though that will always be a matter of opinion – and interesting, allowing us to think about the facts in a new way. These are the only limits that I think should be set on historical interpretation. However, it must be admitted that this view is not shared by all ancient historians. Some argue that very strict limits should be set on the ways in which we interpret our sources; the facts should be allowed to 'speak for themselves', the ancient evidence should not be 'contaminated' with ideas or concepts drawn from outside ancient history or 'distorted' by the personal prejudices of the historian. Others reveal similar attitudes in the way that they actually practise ancient history.

According to this point of view, the context within which we interpret our facts should be more or less contemporaneous with those facts; or, at the very least, it should be an ancient context. To interpret a passage in one of Cicero's speeches, we should first of all set it in the context of the rest of his writings, then look at the works of other writers from the mid-first century BC. Thereafter we can, if we wish, study the speeches of Demosthenes, an Athenian orator of the fourth century BC, since Cicero used him as a model. We can also draw upon the treatise on rhetoric written by Quintilian in the first century AD, since, although he wrote a century after Cicero, he had first-hand experience of the Roman tradition of oratory. What we must not do is make use of modern theories of rhetoric; they are not ancient, and so do not provide an appropriate context for an ancient text. Likewise, if we assume the existence of 'the ancient economy', which remained more or less the same throughout antiquity, we can draw indiscriminately on bits of evidence from any time in a thousand-year period – but any attempt to introduce non-ancient material, whether modern economic theories or comparison with other periods of history, may be condemned as anachronistic and misleading. We shall be accused of ignoring what makes the ancient world different from our own, and of introducing modern ideas and assumptions where they don't belong.

This accusation is entirely true – and entirely unavoidable.

As I argued above, we can come to understand the ancient world (and any other period of history, and any other culture) only through translation, finding equivalents in our language for their words, concepts and ideas. Inevitably, there is a risk of missing something important, or introducing something new by mistake, but this risk is inherent in *every* attempt at understanding the past. There is no essential difference between using the writings of Quintilian to help interpret a passage of Cicero and using, say, the speeches of Churchill or the theories of Jacques Derrida; the first is simply more obvious (and so less interesting), and more widely accepted within ancient history. In either case, we should have to persuade our readers that the connection we are proposing is interesting and plausible, rather than taking it for granted that the first connection is unproblematic and the second is always illegitimate. Indeed, historians who deliberately and explicitly make use of modern theories are likely to be far more careful about what they're doing and far more aware of the potential problems than someone who ostentatiously renounces the use of modern concepts and then unselfconsciously uses a word like 'state', with all its modern overtones, to describe Rome.

We wish to understand Athenian society. There is an entire academic discipline, sociology, devoted to trying to understand how societies work, and it seems quite perverse not to take advantage of this. Alternatively, for those who believe that Athens was radically different from any society in the modern industrialised world, there are anthropological

theories about the workings of 'primitive' societies. In both
cases, we don't use the theories to tell us how it *was* in the
past, but simply how it might have been; they suggest new
ways of thinking about the ancient evidence. The Athenians
were not exactly like modern Westerners, nor exactly like
New Guinea tribesmen, but it is entirely legitimate to argue
that they were sufficiently similar in certain important re-
spects for such comparisons to be worthwhile. If they were
completely alien, if there was no equivalence at all between
our world and theirs, we would be wholly incapable of
understanding anything about them. History involves a constant tension between sameness and difference; we have to
translate antiquity into our terms at the same time as we
emphasise the distance between us and them.

It will always be a matter of opinion whether a particular
approach is plausible or not. For example, someone who
wishes to use Freudian psychoanalysis to interpret Greek
tragedy has to assume both that the Greek mind worked in
more or less the same way as the twentieth-century mind and
also that Freud's analysis of the workings of the human mind
is valid; both ideas are contentious. What is clear, however,
is that there are no valid grounds for ruling that this way of
interpreting the evidence is automatically illegitimate simply
because it uses modern concepts. The historian who tries
(vainly) to exclude all such 'contamination' will not produce
a more objective and reliable piece of history but an inferior,
impoverished interpretation which is entirely at the mercy of
the author's *unconscious* preconceptions and prejudices.

The same may be said of the use of personal experience in interpreting evidence. It is impossible to prevent our thoughts and feelings from colouring our interpretation of the ancient world, and it may even be detrimental to our understanding if we try. For example, someone whose parents divorced messily when she was twelve is likely to have a different view of marriage, including Roman marriage, from someone whose family background is completely stable. Such experiences might just give the first person a special insight into the nature of the ancient family. Of course she can't argue purely on the basis of her personal experience ('I've been through this so my interpretation of the evidence must be right'), but as a result of that experience she may come up with new connections between facts and new ways of looking at old evidence. The risk that she may lose her sense of proportion and become too involved in the subject is surely no greater than in the case of someone who tries to suppress his feelings and believes that his account is free from emotion and personal prejudice.

The converse of this is that when reading the works of other historians it is always worthwhile considering how their personal circumstances may have helped to form their view of the ancient world. The obvious example is that of M.I. Rostovtzeff, the great economic and social historian. Rostovtzeff was a liberal intellectual who was forced out of Russia after the Revolution by the Bolsheviks; he interpreted ancient history in terms of the long struggle between the beleaguered forces of civilisation and culture in the Greek cities and the ignorant peasant masses. The connection is almost painfully obvious. Many historians regard this sort of approach to reading other historians with enormous suspicion, arguing that the writings should be left to speak for themselves. But writings speak for themselves no more than facts do; we have to read and interpret them, and it is entirely legitimate (if not unavoidable) to read historians' work in the light of what we know about their background, political views, prejudices and so forth. It may not make much of a difference to our reading, especially as we rarely know very much about the historians we have to read (and they rarely lead very interesting lives), but it is something that should always be taken into consideration.

A final problem in the interpretation of the facts, given the fragmentary nature of the evidence, is how to fill the gaps in our knowledge. Here we return to the question of the relationship between history and fiction, and the role of the imagination in each genre. Some historians try to reinforce the contrast by emphasising the factual nature of history: historians simply let the facts speak for themselves, they never go beyond the facts or impose their own ideas on the reality of the past. Nonsense, of course: historians use their imaginations all the time, in interpreting facts and devising connections between them. A historical interpretation is a work of creative fiction, imagining how all the different facts might fit together. The problem for historians lies rather in deciding what limits should be set on the use of the imagination, and how an imaginative reconstruction should be assessed.

The first principle is that of economy; historians should not invent any more than is absolutely necessary. If a historical account mentions the actions of an unnamed soldier, the historian is not at liberty to think up a name for him – though a novelist might. An explanation which involves only a small amount of invention (the Pyramids were constructed by the Egyptians, even if we don't have direct evidence for exactly how they did it) is always preferable to one involving a lot of invention (the Pyramids were constructed by entirely hypothetical alien visitors). The second principle is that the historian should be explicit about which parts of an interpretation are hypothetical (which is a more acceptable word than 'invented'), and should provide evidence and argument to support the hypothesis; the novelist can weave fact and fiction seamlessly together.

Many of the inscriptions which have survived to our time are fragmentary; an epigraphist attempts to fill in the missing words and letters by considering the rest of the inscription and also other, similar inscriptions (on the same principle, we are more likely to reconstruct BEWA— OF TH– D–G as 'Beware of the dog' than 'Bewail of thy dig'). The historian has to do something similar with gaps in the evidence, arguing on the basis of inference from other facts (we have no reliable evidence for mortality rates in ancient Rome, but all the sources suggest that it was a very unhealthy place to live) and from other knowledge (other large cities in pre-industrial times certainly had high mortality rates; medical studies show why this should be). Of course, since any such hypothesis depends on a particular interpretation of the evidence, there is no way of proving it to someone who interprets the facts in a different way. To return to our very first example, Syme invented an 'Augustan party', for which there is no direct evidence, because he saw a series of men with similar backgrounds being elected to the consulship under Augustus; other historians believe that the evidence is insufficient to support his hypothesis and that the facts can be explained more economically as simple coincidence.

Interpretation (2)

Finally, we can return to the fragments of amphorae found in the River Saône. Comparison with other amphorae suggests that these should be classified as belonging to the Dressel 1 type; which tells us something about their date (between the mid-second and late first centuries BC), their original contents (wine) and their provenance (Italy: fragments of amphorae of this type have been found at kiln sites there). We can conclude, therefore, that large amounts of wine were moved in amphorae from Italy to France during this period. This fact can then be incorporated into a history of relations between the two countries, or an account of the Italian wine industry, or a survey of ancient trade. Here, however, we encounter a problem. As already noted, the meaning and significance of any fact will vary according to the sort of story being told. This is true not only when stories are being told about different things, but also when different stories are told about the same thing. In other words, two different historians can use the same fact in an account of the same subject, and yet reach completely different conclusions.

Historians make sense of facts by relating them to other facts. However, they don't always do this at the simple level of relating *a* to *b*, *a* to *c* and so forth. More often, they will relate *a* to their general idea of how *b*, *c*, *d* and the rest connect to one another; what might be termed their overall interpretation. Such an interpretation – for example, a historian's ideas about the nature of trade in the ancient world – is in theory built up from lots of small acts of interpretation, making sense of individual facts and how they connect together. In practice, historians (and still more their students) tend to start with the overall interpretation of an earlier historian and gradually modify it in the light of other people's studies, new evidence and their own changing views. (This is essentially what you're being asked to do in a typical history assignment: read these books and comment on their interpretation of the topic.) In theory, every interpretation should be modified constantly, as new evidence is introduced; we make sense of new information by relating it to what we already know, and we revise what we think we know in the light of new information. In practice, since facts do not have a single intrinsic meaning but rather are given meaning in the context of a particular interpretation, it is almost always possible to explain away a fact that seems to be out of step with our preconceived ideas.

Consider two accounts which might be given of the nature of trade in the ancient world. The first is built on a number of accepted facts: the ancient economy was pre-industrial and based above all on agriculture; most people, therefore, had very little surplus income beyond what they needed to feed themselves and their families; transport was very slow and expensive; the wealthy upper classes regarded trade as a degrading occupation. The conclusion is that most people in the ancient world tried to be self-sufficient, producing as much as possible of the things they needed and consuming most of what they produced; therefore there was virtually no long-distance trade in basic goods like corn, wine or pottery. The amphorae from the River Saône might seem to contradict this story. However, if you accept this interpretation, which is based on a wide range of evidence, then you can explain away a single contradictory example – perhaps the amphorae were part of the supplies of the Roman army in Gaul, nothing to do with market trade – or simply play down its significance when compared with all the evidence which supports your point of view.

An alternative story: an individual peasant had only a small amount of money to spare after selling his tiny surplus, but the aggregate surplus of millions of peasants was considerable; transport was certainly expensive, but no more so than in sixteenth-century England, when there was plenty of trade; the upper classes might claim to despise trade, but should we believe them? Besides, that wouldn't stop them selling the produce of their estates to traders, even if they didn't get any further involved. In other words, there's no reason why trade couldn't have taken place, since both supply and demand existed; and the huge numbers of wine amphorae found in the Saône provide clinching proof that it *was* taking place on a significant scale.

These two interpretations are based on the same set of facts; they interpret them completely differently. Each theory is coherent and logically consistent; each 'plays by the rules', citing all the evidence on which the interpretation is based rather than asking the reader to accept the writer's authority without question; each offers a reasonable, economical explanation that fits with what we know of the way the world works (no UFOs or secret conspiracies). Each one tries to incorporate as much of the evidence as possible; each has to explain away some things that don't quite fit, and does so convincingly (if you agree with that particular interpretation) or unconvincingly (if you don't). Furthermore, this is not an exceptionally contentious subject; in almost every area of ancient history you can take your pick from at least two theories, drawing on the same sources to reach radically different conclusions. On what grounds do we choose between these different interpretations?

There are of course plenty of reasons why we end up preferring one theory to another. The problem, for those who continue to insist that history can and should provide a definitive, objective picture of 'how it really was' in the past, is that these reasons are usually personal and subjective. The form in which the historical account is presented may play an important part in persuading us to accept it. Certainly this helps us distinguish between 'proper' history and supposedly more dubious accounts, but we may also be persuaded to choose the interpretation of one 'proper' historian over another because the writer's style is entertaining, or pleasantly informal, or sober and authoritative, or whatever else is our particular taste. Even more important is the structure of the narrative; whether it tells a coherent story, and whether it is the sort of story that we want to read. Modern readers are generally sceptical of accounts which present historical events as a romance (the triumph of Augustus and the dawn of the new Golden Age in Rome) or as a tragedy (the fall of the great Roman Republic); we are more likely to be persuaded by an account which is presented with a measure of irony and distance.

We also need to consider the role played by authority in determining our choice of interpretation. In crude terms, we may be inclined to accept the theories of a senior professor (who does, after all, have many years of experience in the subject, and whose authority has been recognised by other historians) over that of a junior lecturer, let alone an amateur. More importantly, we are likely to follow the lead of our teachers. We may not accept everything that they tell us, but we will absorb a great deal of their point of view without even noticing; not only in lectures, but through the books they set for assignments, the comments they make on work and even just casual conversation. It is hard to believe that any lecturer, however scrupulously he informs his students of all the different theories on offer, can wholly succeed in giving a fair summary of a view with which he completely disagrees. These are the people we have to please with our essays or dissertations; of course they don't want us to become clones, but at the same time we can't disagree with them *too* much. What begins as a conscious effort to please can quickly become an automatic response.

Traditionally, historians have tended to reject any interpretation that is overtly political, on the grounds that the writer has distorted the evidence by introducing modern ideas and preconceptions. In fact, as we have seen, it is not possible for historians wholly to suppress their personal views, on politics or anything else, as they construct their interpretations. We make sense of facts by relating them to the whole of our experience, not just the bits connected directly with ancient history. The difference between, say, a Marxist or feminist historian and a 'let the facts speak' historian is not that one is political and the other is neutral and objective, but that one is overtly and consciously political while the other either doesn't notice or deliberately conceals the extent to which his account, too, reflects his political views. In other words, I don't think it's right to reject an interpretation simply because it has an explicit political agenda. It is certainly legitimate – indeed, absolutely necessary – to criticise accounts on the basis of their political or moral agenda, their assumptions or their language (if it is sexist or racist, for example). Naturally,

this applies to *all* historical accounts, not just those which are
open about their prejudices.

A good interpretation will be able to account for as much
as possible of the existing evidence without having to explain
away too much. It will be internally consistent, and will be
compatible with the rest of our knowledge about the world.
It should be economical, and it should not have to invent too
much; an interpretation which can explain historical events
without reference to extra-terrestrials, occult forces and global
conspiracies is always to be preferred to one which cannot
(but of course that's what they *want* you to think ...). Finally,
a good interpretation should be *interesting*: it should allow us
to look at the ancient world in a new way, and should open
up new questions and debates. When old interpretations are
abandoned, it is not always because they have been disproved
by new evidence. It may simply be that new ways of understanding the evidence are more attractive and more
productive, whereas the old ideas had come to seem sterile
and irrelevant (which is not to say that they might not return
in a different guise when new theories have run out of steam
in their turn).

How to 'do' ancient history

There is no single correct way of interpreting a piece of
evidence or of constructing an interpretation; different
hypotheses will seem more or less convincing to different
historians, for any number of reasons. Clearly, therefore,

there is no single correct way of 'doing' ancient history – but I do believe that there are better and worse ways. Some approaches to the subject produce more interesting or more persuasive interpretations. It should be obvious by now that I have little time for the sort of history that 'lets the facts speak for themselves'. Facts *don't* speak: the historian who tries to listen to nothing but the facts will produce an interpretation that is driven by his own unconscious preconceptions, assumptions and prejudices. Such an account will also be deeply impoverished through his refusal to pay attention to anything going on outside his narrow little field of interest. Such works of scholarship may offer reasonably definitive descriptions of what the sources have to say on a particular subject, and thus provide us with a useful basis for developing our own interpretations. They themselves advance our understanding and offer interesting insights only by accident.

How *should* we do ancient history? No historian would disagree with the idea that we need to read both ancient sources and modern interpretations carefully and critically. We have to remember that the 'facts' are, in both cases, presented to us in the context of a particular interpretation; no account ever offers us just the facts, free from any trace of an argument. To make proper use of these facts, we need first to identify the underlying argument and the assumptions on which it rests. Whatever you do, don't just believe everything you're told; *every* statement should be taken apart and scrutinised before, reluctantly, you accept that it might conceivably be true. Those of you who find it difficult to break the habit of obedience to authority that was so carefully instilled in you in school could try turning to the reviews in journals like *Classical Review, Journal of Hellenic Studies, Journal of Roman Studies, Greece & Rome* and the *Bryn Mawr Classical Review* (published electronically) where you'll often find a ready-made critique of the argument and assumptions of the books on your reading list.

When we write ancient history, we need to be equally critical. We need to know what we're doing, and to tell our readers what we're doing, when we make use of a particular bit of evidence or build up our grand interpretations, rather than behaving as if the whole process is completely natural and unproblematic. We should take nothing for granted; we should certainly not behave as if our interpretations, our assumptions, even our choice of words are somehow given, inherent in the evidence, entirely neutral. *We* select the facts and give them meaning; we make sense of the past by translating it into our terms. However, at the same time as we are forced to abandon the illusion that we can produce an objective account of 'how it really was' in the past, we find that we have gained the freedom to explore any number of different ways of producing *our* account of the past. We do not have to accept the traditional limits on the range of material we can call on in producing our interpretations; anything, from economic theory to pop music to Chinese history, may suggest new ways of looking at the ancient evidence and new ways of thinking about the past.

Perhaps, just perhaps, if we think and write about the process of historical interpretation more carefully and explicitly, we might be able to do it rather better.

CHAPTER 3

Telling the Story

How to begin?

What is the most effective way to begin? What is the most appropriate way? Which one should we be aiming at? Who sets the rules that determine how history ought to be written? Are these generic conventions simply a matter of convenience, or tradition, or do they serve some other purpose? How far does the form of a book determine the way in which we set about reading it – for example, whether we approach it as history or as fiction? How far are historical narratives determined by the facts, and how far by conventions of story-telling or the artistic imagination of historians? What difference does it make to your reading of a chapter if it begins with a set of questions rather than a series of factual statements or assertions? How should *we* write ancient history?

History is a particular kind of story, and so clearly it is possible for us to study a historical account *as a story*, looking at its narrative structure, its style, its language and so forth. Traditionally, historians have regarded literary technique as an optional extra: what *really* matters in history is the content of the work, not the form in which it is presented. Language is seen as a tool, simply the means for conveying a message. However, many modern theorists argue that language is not so 'transparent', that the *way* in which we say something forms part of the message and therefore affects the meaning. A passage which claims to be giving you a simple outline of the argument is actually doing something more complex, trying to persuade you to carry on reading ('if you don't, you won't see how I develop these arguments'), telling you how to read the chapter ('*these* are the issues you should be worrying about') and setting its tone (pedantic, chatty, authoritative, blustering, whatever). Titles do the same sort of thing: 'Snappy and Eye-Catching Phrase: rather tedious summary of actual subject matter, 200 BC - AD 200'.

As Hayden White argued over twenty years ago, 'In general there has been a reluctance to consider historical narratives as what they most manifestly are: verbal fictions, the contents of which are as much *invented* as *found* and the forms of which have more in common with their counterparts in literature than they have with those in the sciences'.[1] In other words, history is a kind of story, it has much in common with other kinds of story (including myths, and fiction), and studying it *as a story* can tell us something about the way in which the historical account 'works'.[2] White's pioneering writings have returned repeatedly to this topic, and the theme of this chapter is neatly summed up by the titles of two of his works: 'the historical text as literary artifact' and 'the content of the form'.[3]

'In those years, it seems to have been the fashion to think that only a particularly austere and even repulsive style of writing could entitle the historian to the name of scholar.' Professor Elton smiled grimly, his tongue flickering out to wipe away the caustic aftertaste of that final word. So much for Tait and Pollard, and anyone else for whom dullness was the cardinal virtue of historical writing! The titles of their books, the opening sentences, the very typeface, all proclaimed their ivory-tower elitism and smug superiority. To hell with the pack of them! Yet there was danger too from the opposite extreme: what of those who might accept *no* limits on the exercise of the historian's creative powers, not even those of strict factual accuracy and verifiability? The rules of the game must be enforced – fact is fact, fiction is fiction – or the entire historical establishment was doomed to contempt and derision. Once more Elton took up his pen, oblivious to the encroaching shadows.

I first began to think consciously about the rhetoric of historical writing back in 1994, when I gave a couple of lectures on historical theory as part of a course for ancient historians in the Department of Classics at Lampeter (University of Wales). When, I found myself wondering, was it acceptable to use the word 'I' in history? Professors could do it all the time; junior lecturers might do it in lectures but never in their books or articles (except in prefaces or acknowledgements); students seemed to be discouraged from expressing any opinion of their own whatsoever. In retrospect, it is rather alarming that it had taken me so long to start worrying about such things. When I talk of students who become so good at imitating the accepted style and approach of 'proper' ancient history that they start to take these conventions entirely for granted, I am thinking, first and foremost, of myself. It still feels strange, even uncomfortable, to say 'I think' rather than 'it is clear that ...'.

Narrative

All historical accounts involve some element of narrative; that is, the description of a series of events that are connected to one another causally and chronologically. Some consist almost entirely of narrative: most biographies of emperors or other ancient figures, most books with titles or subtitles like *A History of the Greek World/ the Roman Republic/ the English-Speaking Peoples/ Whatever*. The majority of ancient historical works take this form; Thucydides' account of the Peloponnesian War, Livy's history of Republican Rome and so forth.[4] The aim of such accounts is to tell a story about the past, to recount significant events in the 'life' of their subject, whether a state, a people, a war or a person. Passages of description or analysis are generally short, and subordinate to the 'action'; they are introduced to provide background information for the reader (how the Roman political system worked) or to explain in more detail why events took a particular turn (how Marius managed to get himself re-elected as consul).

   At the other end of the spectrum are historical accounts

whose aim is primarily analytical or descriptive, in which narrative plays only a minor role. JACT's *The World of Athens*, for example, offers a brief survey of 'significant events' at the beginning, but concentrates on providing a description of different aspects of life in Athens during the fifth and fourth centuries BC; it is less like a story, more like a detailed character sketch. A work of analysis like M.I. Finley's *The Ancient Economy* contains no narrative whatsoever. A major part of Finley's argument is that the nature of the economy did not change in any significant way during the whole of antiquity; it is clear, therefore, that any attempt to offer a narrative account of its development would be entirely point-less.

Although most of the classics of historical writing over the centuries have been narrative accounts, today narrative is generally regarded as an unsophisticated and inferior form of history. Of course you have to determine what happened in the past (the main aim of narrative) before you can discuss why it happened, but establishing a narrative framework is now seen precisely as necessary preparation for the tasks of analysis and interpretation rather than as an end in itself. Narrative history is (arguably) superficial, concentrating on short-term events rather than looking deeper at the struc-tures that determined the course of events; moreover, it offers a misleading and politically dubious vision of a past dominated by the political and military activities of upper-class men. Narrative is for schoolchildren and the general public; *real* historians consider themselves above merely telling a story. As the sorts of questions set for assignments and exams show, university students are expected to behave like 'real' historians. You shouldn't answer a question on how Augustus rose to power by giving a narrative of significant events but by constructing an analytical argument, discussing the various factors involved in his success and trying to decide which was the most important.

Nevertheless, however much modern historians may despise narrative, they cannot escape it altogether. Narrative provides the indispensable framework for historical analysis. We don't study a subject like slavery in a timeless void, we study Greek slavery or slavery in Italy in the second century BC; slavery at a particular time or place, in the context of a period or a century – in other words, in the context of a chronological framework that tells us, at the very least, that Greek slavery comes before Roman slavery and that both were roughly two thousand years before our own time. In practice, I think this chronological framework tells us much more; our understanding of a period is shaped by the narratives that tell us how it relates to other periods and to the modern day. When we consider a subject 'in context', most of that context is provided by the narrative framework – not only the traditional narratives of political events, though they still tend to dominate our ideas about what constitutes or characterises a 'period' of history, but other sorts of narrative as well.

For example: as I've mentioned, Finley can exclude narrative from his account of the ancient economy because he

doesn't think that there were any significant changes in the
nature of the economy over the whole period of antiquity.
However, clearly there have been major changes in the
economy *since* antiquity. While he doesn't discuss it explicitly,
it is clear that Finley thinks about the ancient economy in the
context of a grand narrative of the development of society
from antiquity through the middle ages to the modern world.
This narrative argues that there was a dramatic change in the
organisation of society at the end of the middle ages, as a
result of which the modern world is in every respect different
from earlier societies. It explains this change in terms of
changes in patterns of thought (the development of modern
economic rationality and the 'Protestant work ethic'), which
affected human behaviour and hence shaped the rest of
society. Finley interprets the ancient evidence in the light of
this overall interpretation of human history and the dynamics
of historical change. In other words, the conclusions of his
analysis of the ancient economy are determined, at least in
part, by the narrative framework within which he works.

Most 'proper' historians steer well clear of attempts to
construct narratives of the whole of human history or to
reveal the underlying logic of historical development. The
common faults of this sort of speculative 'philosophy of
history' – a cavalier attitude to evidence, a love of sweeping
generalisations, the blatantly ideological nature of its conclusions – are so utterly at odds with good historical practice.
And yet, as we've seen with Finley, historians cannot escape
the influence of such narratives on their own interpretations

of the past. I've suggested before that history involves a
constant tension between sameness and difference, making
sense of the past in our own terms but also emphasising the
distance between our world and that of antiquity. We may see
the differences between present and past in terms of mental-
ity, or technology, or the organisation of society. We may
argue (as Finley does) that there is a fundamental qualitative
difference between now and then, or we may believe that the
differences are simply a matter of scale. The point is that each
of these perspectives rests on a different philosophy of
history: a different interpretation of what drives historical
change, a different narrative of what happened between
antiquity and our own time. The problem is not that historians are dependent on such narratives, but that most of them
are quite unconscious of this, or believe that they can successfully avoid any such 'contamination' of the evidence.

You may have noticed a certain amount of slippage between the terms 'narrative' and 'interpretation' in this
discussion. This is quite deliberate: while an interpretation of
a period of history (or of history as a whole) may be presented either as an analytical argument or as a narrative, every
narrative account of the past is an interpretation. Historians
do not 'find' narratives in the ancient evidence by 'revealing'
the connections between events. On the contrary, it is the
historians who construct narratives by deciding which events
should be included, how they should be interpreted and how
they may be shown to be connected to one another. The
story is not inherent in the events, since clearly the same

event can be incorporated into many different stories (just as
the same fact can be interpreted in many different ways). At
most, an event constitutes a 'story element', which the historian combines with other elements to create a narrative.

The crucial difference between an analytical account and a
narrative account lies in the form in which the historical
interpretation is presented, and the way in which the form of
the account works to persuade the reader to accept the
historian's interpretation of the past. The persuasiveness of
an analytical account of a period of history rests on the
coherence and plausibility of its argument. The evidence on
which the argument is based and the way in which the
historian has interpreted this evidence (and even, in many
cases, alternative ways of interpreting it) are described in
detail.[5] A narrative account is far more subtle and slippery.
Its explanatory power, its capacity to persuade, rests not on
any explicit argument but on its success in telling a convincing story. The account is judged above all on the basis of the
selection of events to be included and the ways in which they
are shown to be connected. Clearly all of this does depend
on the historian's subjective interpretations of the evidence,
but it is not presented as such. Rather, the narrative claims
simply to recount what happened in the past.

What, then, makes a convincing story? Hayden White,
who has written extensively on the subject of historical
narratives, draws on the work of literary critics who argue
that there are a limited number of basic story forms, basic
plots, in our culture. Stories can, according to this view, be

classified according to whether their plot structure is that of romance, comedy, tragedy or satire.[6] White suggests that the historian comes to the evidence with an idea of the sorts of stories that might be told about it – in other words, these archetypal plot structures. Historical narratives thus tend to be plotted in terms of romance, comedy etc. The reader has the same awareness of what constitutes a proper story (in our culture, at least; other cultures may favour different story forms) and judges the historical narrative accordingly. Different historians and different readers will prefer one story form over another (especially as White argues that each of the different plot structures is associated with a particular political stance). They will therefore interpret historical events (and reject certain accounts of those events) accordingly. Finally, White implies that the popularity of different plot structures in society as a whole will vary over time. We might say, for example, that the Victorians had a very Romantic view of history as progress, whereas we tend to see history in more Satirical terms, as a succession of events which cannot be understood in terms of any monolithic Grand Narrative.

This argument may become clearer if we consider an example: how might we construct a narrative of the fall of the Roman Republic and the rise of Augustus?[7] There are plenty of possibilities. We might begin with the birth of Octavian and chart his struggles to claim his rightful inheritance and save Rome from civil war (a very Romantic view). We might instead begin much earlier, in the second or even the third century BC and show how the Republic was brought down

by the selfish actions of men like Caesar and Pompey and/or
by its own flaws (the Tragic perspective). We might follow
the events of the Civil Wars but conclude with Augustus
restoring the Republic in 28/7 BC; despite the period of
upheaval, order is restored and everything ends happily
(Comedy). Finally, we might take any one of these stories and
undermine it, turning it into satire: a tragic account of the
Republic's demise that ends not with the death of Cicero but
with the elevation of his son to the consulship in 30 BC, or
an account of Augustus' career which emphasises the gap
between his public persona and his actual deeds.

Each of these stories offers a different interpretation of
the final years of the Republic. They are based on different
views of the best way to study the subject (should we concentrate on the actions of a single man, or on longer-term
causes?) and on different interpretations of particular events
(do we believe that Augustus was sincere in 'restoring the
Republic'?). When we come to read these narratives, however, we need to take account not only of these individual
acts of interpretation but also of the story as a whole; is it the
sort that we find convincing, the sort we want to hear? For
example, I myself have no time whatsoever for the Romantic
view of history as a heroic quest, whether focused on an
individual (Augustus, Alexander) or an institution (the inevitable triumph of Christianity over paganism). This sort of
story does not ring true to me; I just don't think that history
works like that. Since the evidence is always open to different

interpretations, I am free to reject such accounts as a matter
of course.

This is an entirely personal, subjective opinion. Someone
who holds a more romantic view of history as a whole would
be more readily convinced that an individual episode should
be understood in romantic terms. They could certainly reject
my anti-romantic interpretation on the grounds that it's
based on arbitrary assumptions about the way that history
works (so is their interpretation, of course, but we always
tend to take our own assumptions for granted as universal
truths). This does raise a problem for those who argue that
historians can show 'how it really was'. We judge historical
accounts on the basis of the plausibility of their interpretation
of the ancient evidence – but our idea of what constitutes a
plausible interpretation is dependent on our general philosophy of history, and what that tells us about the sorts of stories
we can expect to find in the past. How, then, do we decide
between different philosophies of history? We may choose
on the basis of whether we find their interpretations of
history convincing (but how do we judge their plausibility,
except on the basis of pre-existing assumptions about the
nature of history?); we may make our choice on political
grounds (which is one of the reasons why I don't like the
Romantic view of history). However, our choice must surely
be determined in part also by unconscious motivations, by
the results of social conditioning (as mentioned above, different societies tend to prefer certain kinds of story) and by
our own personal psychology (do we want a story that

excites, terrifies, reassures, unsettles, amuses or devastates us?). Ultimately, the question of what sort of story we find (or want to find) in the past is surely inextricably linked to the question of why stories about the past should be important to us in the first place, a question that I shall discuss in the next chapter.

We will have reasons for preferring some kinds of stories to others, but is there any limit to the number of stories that can be told about the same historical events? Theoretically, no: there is no story inherent in the events, so they can potentially be emplotted in any number of different ways. In practice, of course there are limits. An individual historian will tend to emplot events in a limited number of ways; I could write an account of the life of Augustus in romantic terms as a technical exercise, but I wouldn't present that sort of account as history because I simply don't think it was like that. More importantly, limits are set by the fact that the historian is a member of a profession and a member of society, and tends to conform to the standards and expectations of each of these groups. For example: I imagine that it is theoretically possible to emplot the Holocaust as a comedy rather than a tragedy (the usual version), but the assumptions you would have to make about the value of Jewish lives would be utterly objectionable to most if not all historians and at least the majority of the rest of the population.[8] In our society, such a narrative is simply not acceptable. However, it is salutary to think that such an account might have become the standard version of events if the Nazis had won the war.

History is written, at least initially, by the victors: think of the accounts of the coming of civilisation to the American West that can present their subject in romantic terms precisely by devaluing the lives of the Native Americans who were slaughtered to make way for civilisation.[9]

The main concern for historians is the question of what sorts of stories can be told about the past. Narrative is not a problem; it is simply an inextricable part of what they do. Indeed, there might be a case for arguing that it is the most important part. Narrative structures shape our understanding of a period and hence our interpretation of the evidence. The main purpose of analysis, it might be argued, is to enable us to produce more detailed narratives (for example, to give us a better understanding of the background to the Gracchan crisis) or to write new ones (a broad narrative of economic and social change in the Roman Republic, of which the Gracchan crisis was merely a surface symptom). We have to ask, therefore, why so many modern historians reject the narrative approach to history. In part, it seems, they reject it on methodological grounds ('God is in the details'); in part for political reasons, reacting against the obvious faults of traditional narrative history. One important factor seems to be the question of the form of the different accounts, which can help to mark out history from other sorts of writing. Analytical history imitates the style and approach of hard, factual, 'scientific' subjects like sociology, whereas narrative might seem alarmingly similar to fiction – not least in its basic purpose of telling a story. Finally, I suspect, it is simply that it is more difficult to write a good narrative account than a good analytical account; narrative requires broad historical vision and literary ability on top of all the usual skills of historical analysis. If you can obtain a list of my previous publications, you will note that I have not yet tried my hand at narrative....

Voice

Who speaks to us in the historical text? What difference does it make to the way that we read it? Most historical accounts are presented in the third person: 'Themistocles persuaded the Greeks to halt the fleet near Salamis; an engagement with the Persians thus became inevitable.' The narrator is omniscient, impersonal and objective: this is simply how things were (even ideas based on an interpretation of the evidence – for example, that the battle was inevitable – are presented as statements of fact). Sometimes, when the state of the evidence does not permit such absolute certainty, we find instead the impersonal third person passive: 'It is clear that', 'it is likely that'. Once again, the voice of authority states the facts – this *is* the most plausible interpretation of the evidence – and it takes a certain amount of nerve to disagree, or to point out that other interpretations are perfectly possible.

Sometimes, the first person plural is used: 'We may now turn to another important question.' Historian and reader are on a journey of discovery, they investigate the problem together. Of course, it is the historian who determines the course of the research and decides what the conclusion will be, but perhaps readers will be more inclined to accept the historian's conclusions if they are treated like equals and made to feel part of things. This approach does at least acknowledge that the audience are not wholly passive, seeking merely to be told what to believe, but it offers only the appearance of active involvement in the investigation of the past. The historian remains in control, presenting personal interpretations as what 'we' know or what 'we' have discovered. At the same time, by highlighting the process by which 'we' increase our knowledge of past events, the historian emphasises the 'scientific', analytical nature of history – in contrast to a fictional account of the past, which presents a seamless account of events.

Most of the above statements could, or indeed should, be expressed in the first person singular: 'I think that' rather than 'it is clear that', 'I will now tell you about' rather than 'let us now look at'. After all, there is one person, the historian, expounding his or her personal interpretation of the evidence to an audience. However, as you have probably noticed by now, historians very rarely write 'I' (except in the acknowledgements, where it doesn't really count). They may *say* it more frequently, for example in lectures, and so it does appear in books based on lectures such as Finley's *Ancient Economy*. Particularly eminent professors (the sort who get invited to give prestigious lectures which are then published) seem to have greater freedom to admit to having opinions, since their opinions are considered authoritative on the basis of their vast knowledge and experience. The rest present their personal interpretation of the evidence as if it was incontrovertible fact, or at any rate the only conclusion that any reasonable person could reach. This is how it was, not just how I think it was.

This is less of a problem for the reader – once she realises that, regardless of the form in which they are presented, historical accounts are based on subjective, personal inter-pretations and should be treated as such – than it is for the historians themselves. Some historians write like this because they genuinely believe that their account of the past is com-pletely objective and factual. A few, perhaps, consciously adopt this tone as the best way of persuading readers to accept their personal conclusions. The majority of historians write like this because they learn, early in their training, that this is how you are supposed to write history. This is the accepted tone of professional historical writing: if you want to get decent essay marks, or pass your PhD, or get your book or article published, you should try to mimic this style. It shows that you belong to the club, or are serious about wishing to join; it marks you out as a proper historian whose views are to be taken seriously. If you try to speak in a different voice, your views may not be taken so seriously. No wonder that most historians choose to conform. Most inter-nalise the rules of historical discourse to the extent that they become second nature.

What function do these conventions serve? They help to distinguish history from other sorts of writing about the past, and to reinforce history's claim to authority. Historians may not actually be able to offer a completely objective, scientific account of the past, but by adopting the voice of the impersonal, omniscient narrator they can create that impression. The prestige of the historical account might be undermined if it was seen to depend on the subjective interpretations of the historian rather than on solid, objective fact; if historians cannot exclude the personal from the process of interpretation, they must at least exclude any overt signs of this from their accounts. They should present the past as it was, not the past as it seems to them. Accounts which are too obviously personal can be dismissed purely on the grounds that they are not conforming to the accepted mode of historical discourse. Cynically, one might suggest that they are excluded because they don't even try to pretend to be objective; because they give the game away.

What's wrong with the traditional style of historical writing? I can think of at least two reasons why it might be a problem. First, and most obviously, it's a fraud; the historical account cannot present the past 'as it really was', so why pretend that it can? Secondly, there is something very disturbing about the idea that people should suppress their personalities and personal views and speak only in a certain way. Moreover, the voice of traditional scholarly discourse, which we are supposed to mimic, is not as neutral and impersonal as it claims. It is the voice of academia: the voice of educated white middle-class privilege and of male authority. Of course, a high proportion of ancient historians *are* white middle-class males, and so presumably don't have too much of a problem adapting to the prevailing mode of discourse (although they may still resent the fact that they are not allowed to express themselves in their own idiom). But as for women, non-whites, the working classes and everyone else, they are to be judged on the basis of whether they can mimic the voice of the elite. They are denied a voice of their own.

My main argument in this chapter is that the traditional forms of historical discourse are not natural or inevitable. They serve an ulterior purpose; above all, to reinforce the authority of the particular historical account and of history in general. Most importantly, there is no reason why they cannot be changed. I don't think that I can show the past 'as it really was', so I don't see why I should have to talk as if I can. I am happy to highlight my role in presenting an image of the past (and have as a result had one article rejected on the grounds that sections were 'too personal' – I'm almost as proud about this as I am irritated). By adopting a more personal voice, I hope to elicit a different response from you, the reader; to persuade you to engage with these issues as if I was presenting them to you in conversation, or at any rate in a fairly relaxed seminar, rather than in a lecture. Yes, of course it's a very one-sided conversation, in which I retain total control over the subject matter and the course of the argument. Yes, of course it's a rhetorical technique, designed to persuade you to accept my arguments – but *any* attempt at

communication is unavoidably rhetorical, and is no less trustworthy because of that.

What I want to emphasis is that you do have a choice.
Perhaps I should say rather that you *should* have a choice; it
is a fact that, as things currently stand, anyone who tries to
deviate from the accepted forms of historical writing line
runs the risk of losing marks or having her work rejected. In
an ideal world, however, you would have the freedom to
express yourself in whatever voice best suited your purpose.
Some historians wish to be able to speak in the first person,
to talk about what they think or feel about the past; others
(Gibbon and Syme, for example) can express their personalities quite adequately through traditional third-person
narratives.[10] Some feel oppressed by the dominant mode of
discourse and try to oppose it by offering alternative voices;
others are happy to subvert the system from within, using the
dominant mode of discourse to dissect the structures of
power that it was supposed to maintain.[11] In the future, all
these voices may be heard and listened to. At present, most
historical writing speaks in the monolithic voice of the academy: white, male, middle-class, middle-aged. No wonder so
few people outside the academy are listening.

Rhetoric

The adoption of an impersonal narrative voice is only one of
the conventions that govern historical writing and mark it off
clearly from other sorts of writing about the past. We can,

most of the time, recognise that we're reading a work of history rather than of fiction, or vice versa, on the basis of the style in which it is written rather than its content. This is not to say that all historical accounts are written in exactly the same way, but they do all have to adhere to certain generic conventions if they are to be classified as history and treated as such. As we've seen in the case of voice, these conventions are a means of policing the boundaries of history, identifying certain works as proper history and rejecting those which do not conform. In addition, they work to evoke particular responses from the reader, to create certain impressions or effects; above all, to persuade the reader to accept the historian's personal interpretation of the past as an exact picture of 'how it really was'. They constitute the rhetoric of historical discourse.

Rhetoric, the art of using language so as to persuade others, has often been regarded with suspicion. The Athenian comic playwright Aristophanes caricatured it as the art of making the worse argument appear the better. Rhetoric is contrasted with plain, honest speech; it is exaggerated, artificial, false; it is dangerous, because it can persuade people to make decisions on the basis of appearances rather than reality. In fifth- and fourth-century Athens, where public speaking and debate were central to the workings of democracy, rhetoric could be seen as a threat to the well-being of the state. Similar concerns have been voiced in modern times in response to the rise of 'image politics', the triumph of style and soundbites over substance. However, the implication of

such complaints is that it is possible to communicate in a way
that is free from any trace of rhetoric. On the contrary, any
use of language is inevitably at some level rhetorical. The
'plain speaker' simply employs a different rhetorical strategy
from the impassioned orator; one designed to create the
appearance (which may or may not correspond to reality) of
straightforwardness, honesty and common sense. Those (like
the anti-democratic philosopher Plato) who ostentatiously
reject rhetoric (itself a rhetorical strategy) are often those who
know what is good for the state and who would rather not
have to bother with the messy and unpredictable business of
persuading other people to accept their point of view.

All historical accounts are rhetorical. Like narrative, rhetoric is not a problem for historians; it is simply part of what
they do. The problem for writers of history is rather with
their choice of particular rhetorical strategies, and with the
limits set on that choice by historical convention. Readers,
meanwhile, need to be sensitive to the rhetorics of historians,
adopting a critical attitude not only towards their statements
and arguments but also towards the form in which these are
presented. We've already seen how, consciously or unconsciously, the use of an omniscient third-person narrative
presents the historian's personal interpretation of the past as
an exact picture of 'how it really was'. We can examine other
aspects of the traditional rhetoric of historical writing, and
see how they are used for the purpose of persuading the
reader to accept the historian's account as true and reliable.

Consider, for example, the effect created by a particular

choice of vocabulary. 'Caligula exhibited symptoms of considerable mental disturbance'; 'Caligula was clearly off his
head'. The first sentence is ostentatiously scholarly, precise
and carefully nuanced; it treats Caligula's mental state as a
serious object of serious study. Of course, we might also find
this sentence ponderous and pompous, especially in certain
contexts; someone who came out with such a phrase in
conversation or even in a lecture might become an object of
derision unless they made it clear that they were speaking
ironically or sarcastically. The second sentence, meanwhile,
is forthright, conversational and deliberately vulgar, treating
its subject as a matter of amusement. We might prefer this
direct, populist approach, but it is clearly not the accepted
style of historical writing. The crucial question is whether
these sentences are actually saying different things. Is the first
sentence framed in those terms to make a very precise point,
or to show off the writer's superior education? Is the second
sentence not acceptable because such a limited vocabulary is
inadequate to express the complexities of the subject, or
simply because it shows that the writer is not quite one of us,
not playing the game? In other words, do historians *have* to
speak like that to make their meaning clear, or does their
choice of words serve some other purpose?

Inevitably, the answer is a mixed one. Historians need to
be able to describe complex and unfamiliar objects, institutions and processes as accurately as possible. They also want
to convey to the reader a sense of what the past was like, to
express the unknown in terms of the known. They therefore

need to call on all the resources of the language in their search for the right word, or *mot juste*. But at the same time, clearly, language functions as a mark of social identity; the way that I speak can reveal my class, my level of education and my background, as well as my membership of a particular group or groups (most obviously, whether I talk like a proper ancient historian). The accepted language of history is the discourse of the elite, emphasising superior education, knowledge and authority. It insists upon refinement, good breeding and ironic understatement, as a means of maintaining social distinctions; you should say 'excrement' or 'faeces', not 'shit'. It is notable that historians, in their attempts to evoke the past, can call on the whole range of English vocabulary except for the vernacular.

Language is both a means of communication and an instrument of obfuscation and oppression. The problem for historians is that their desire for accuracy, which leads them to make use of an extensive vocabulary, can all too easily make their writing seem elitist and exclusive, inaccessible to anyone outside a narrow circle of experts. This is most obvious in the case of 'jargon', excessively technical or specialised language. The positive case for jargon – the reason why we sometimes need to use it – is that technical terms operate as a form of shorthand within a group. Take the word *polis*, for example. The Greek cannot be translated into English without obscuring part of what the word meant in the original. Modern books therefore tend to transliterate rather than translate the word, using it as a specialised term which experienced historians will understand. Theoretical 'jargon' from other disciplines works in the same way; words like 'mimesis', 'alienation' or 'post-Fordism' are readily intelligible to people with some background knowledge of the subject in question. Of course it's perfectly possible to explain all these concepts in 'plain, simple English', but it takes time; for discussion within the group, it's much easier to use the shorthand.

Difficulties arise when historians or other specialists attempt to communicate with those who don't share their knowledge, assumptions and vocabulary. This is a particular problem when a historian wants to use technical terms from another discipline, like sociology or economics, to talk about some aspect of the past. Other historians won't necessarily be familiar with these terms, and may also object to their use on the grounds that this is imposing modern theories on the past. Jargon can thus hinder or even prevent communication, even when the writer is simply trying to find the most useful and appropriate words for describing the past. Jargon can certainly be used in this way deliberately: to exclude from discussion people who don't share the same theoretical assumptions or to enhance the status of the writer as possessor of a superior understanding beyond the comprehension of the ignorant masses. On the other hand, we shouldn't go along with attempts to condemn all jargon, since in practice this invariably means outlawing only the sorts of terms used by people whose theoretical positions are opposed to ours.

Our specialised technical terms are of course indispensable for a proper understanding of the subject ....

Historians employ a certain vocabulary because they feel it is the most effective means of communicating their message, trying to strike the right balance between technical accuracy and accessibility. At the same time, their choice of language sets a particular tone. History books are serious, scholarly, authoritative; they are not supposed to be frivolous, eccentric, confused or vulgar. Historians present the past using the language of the expert who possesses superior knowledge. They sometimes adopt the language of the scientist, the most prestigious sort of expert in our culture (occasionally even going to the lengths of numbering their paragraphs 2.2, 2.3 etc.). Lengthy sentences and complex sentence structure emphasise their superior education; obscure references and allusions, long and incomprehensible footnotes, interminable citations of other learned texts, all of these create an impression of their great knowledge and experience.[12] The style of their writing insists that their views *must* be taken seriously.

This can be seen above all in the attitude of most historians towards the use of metaphor and other figures of speech in their writing. In the traditional mode of historical writing, the highest stylistic virtues are clarity and accuracy. Historians are not expected to display literary skill, to write vividly or poetically or beautifully. The interest of their accounts should lie in the content, not the way in which they are written. The historian aims to use language literally, to describe a separate, objective reality (the past) as accurately as possible. Figurative language, describing things in terms of other things, is associated with fiction and hence falsity, or at the very least subjectivity. Even if an event in a novel is described by an omniscient, impersonal narrator, rather than through the eyes of a character, it is still clearly the novelist's impression, not a description of objective reality. However, we have already questioned the idea that the historian is able to uncover the objective reality of the past. From this perspective, we might consider the possibility that the historian's use of literal, non-figurative language is designed to create the impression that what is being described is real, not just an interpretation.

In fact, all language is figurative. We constantly describe things in terms of other things, but simply don't notice most of the time that we're doing it. The literal, non-figurative language of history is not free from metaphors; it is simply that most of the metaphors are 'dead', and so we no longer recognise them as figures of speech. Think of the words which historians most often use to describe change: development, growth, evolution, decay. All of these are metaphors, comparing change in an institution or a society to change in a living organism or a species. We can talk of the birth of Athenian democracy and the decline and fall of the Roman Empire without necessarily being aware that we're not talking literally, and certainly without worrying about it very much. This is not a problem; it is simply the way that language works. The problem is that historians persist in

believing that they can describe the past without recourse to
figures of speech, and so make use only of dead metaphors
which have become so familiar that we take them for granted.

Figures of speech help us to understand the world by
describing the unfamiliar in terms of the familiar (comparing
change over decades or centuries with the sorts of change
which we know well – the alternation of day and night, the
cycle of the seasons or the course of a human life) and by
making us think of the familiar in a new way by comparing it
with something else. However, the figures of speech we use
to describe something can also come to restrict the way that
we think about it; the metaphor becomes stale and no longer
aids our understanding. In the nineteenth century, the metaphor of 'evolution' radically altered the way that people
viewed the past; it is now little than a synonym for 'change',
with the vague implication that it is change towards a better
or more sophisticated state. The idea of evolution is too
familiar, over-used to the point where it has become almost
meaningless. Certainly it no longer inspires new insights into
the nature of historical change.

Figurative language is indispensable to understanding. The
real question for the historian is not whether societies literally
evolve, but whether thinking about them in these terms is
actually helpful. If the metaphor increases our understanding
or suggests new ways of looking at the past, all well and good.
If not, then we need a new vocabulary, a new set of metaphors, to help us think about change in a new way. Instead
of thinking of society as an organism or a species, we might

think of it as a machine, or an idea, or a recipe, or a game, and consider the implications for our understanding. In our society, science is more prestigious than cookery, and so we are likely to find an attempt to understand history in terms of chaos theory more convincing than an interpretation based on an analogy with jam-making.[13] However, we should not conclude from this that the first approach is more literal or realistic than the second; both are figurative, although the second may *seem* more literary and hence less acceptable in a serious historical account.

The accepted style of historical writing, realism, rests on the assumption that by avoiding overt use of figurative language and other 'literary' traits the historian can provide a true, literal representation of the past as it really was. As we've seen, it's impossible to separate the 'real' past from historians' interpretations and representations of it. Moreover, realist language is still figurative and literary, still dependent on metaphor and other figures of speech. It may well seem more realistic and true to life, but it is no more an exact representation of reality than other, less realistic styles of representation. I have always found it useful to think of this in terms of an analogy with painting. Consider how different artists might attempt to represent a landscape. The realist tries to reproduce the landscape exactly; the impressionist tries to reproduce the immediate sensory experience of viewing the landscape, the cubist tries to reproduce its essence by reducing it to geometric figures, the surrealist tries to change the viewer's perceptions through a series of unexpected juxtapositions, and so forth. None of these is the 'real' landscape. The realist picture is the most realistic, in the sense that it tries to reproduce accurately what is there, but that is not to say that it provides the truest representation. Viewers may decide, for example, that impressionism gives a better sense of the *experience* of viewing a landscape. Paintings give us, not the landscape itself, but the artist's perception of it. We may prefer some perspectives to others (and realism is still a popular form), but we cannot argue that there is only one correct way of seeing.

The same can be said of literary representations. Realism continues to be an enormously popular style, but it is clearly not the only way of representing the world. We can choose also from surrealism, absurdism, magic realism, existentialism, various other strains of modernism (including the 'stream of consciousness' approach found in Woolf and Joyce) and any number of post-modern approaches. Each of these literary styles had something to offer, some new way of viewing and talking about the world and people's perceptions of it – and history ignored them all. The basic model for historical writing remains nineteenth-century realism; its chosen aim remains the search for and description of a real past. The idea that there may be as many historical representations of the past as there are views of a landscape may, reluctantly, be conceded. It is, after all, so obvious that different historians have found different things in the past (though whether these different representations are considered to be equally valid is quite another matter). The idea that we might then use different techniques of representation in our accounts to bring out different aspects of the past – what might be termed the case for surrealist history – is not accepted.

How much scope is there for changing the way that history is written? This seems to depend partly on our view of history and its purpose: quite simply, why does anyone want to read this stuff? If what we seek is a true account of how it really was in the past, then it is understandable that historians should continue to present their accounts in the way they do. We still tend to assume that realism has a privileged relationship with reality, and hence a realist account is taken to be a trustworthy account. To admit the personal voice into historical writing, or to open up uncertainty, or to use too much figurative language, would undermine the authority of the historian and of history. If, on the other hand, we look to history for something else – for new stories, new ways of seeing the past, new perspectives – then there should be plenty of scope for change. Historians have traditionally concentrated on changing our perceptions of the past through the content of their accounts, by finding new evidence or putting forward new interpretations of the evidence. But we can also experiment with different techniques of representation – figurative language, characterisation, narrative voice, plot structure, even the physical appearance of the text – to see how these too may alter our perceptions of the past.

The end

Here is your answer. Comfort, reassurance, the satisfaction of the desire to know. Everything has been resolved; no more questions. Closure.

But surely the end of questions is the end of history? Is this really what we want? But, if so, how can we ever conclude, except with more questions?

Notes

1. (1978), 82; cf. ibid. (1987); Jenkins, op. cit.

2. White's concern is with the structure of historical narratives; he has less to say about the rhetoric of historical discourse, including the interminable citation of authorities as a smokescreen behind which the author's own views can shelter: cf. e.g. R. Barthes, 'The discourse of history', *Comparative Criticism* 3 (1981); R.H. Brown, *A Poetic for Sociology: towards a logic of discovery for the social sciences* (Cambridge, 1977); J.S. Nelson, A. Megill & D.N. McCloskey, eds, *The Rhetoric of the Human Sciences: language and argument in scholarship and public affairs* (Madison, WI, 1987); M. Shanks, *Classical Archaeology of Greece: experiences of a discipline* (London, 1996), ch. 4. Aren't I well read?

3. Unfortunately, many of White's writings, especially the classic *Metahistory* (Baltimore, 1973), are rather heavy going. For summaries and discussion of his ideas, see Keith Jenkins' *On 'What is History?'* (London, 1995). There you are, notes *can* be helpful.

4. It is interesting to note that the ancient historians who don't place so much emphasis on traditional forms of narrative, writers such as Herodotus (account of Persian Wars constantly interrupted by lengthy passages on barbarian customs, natural history and any old story he picked up in a Halicarnassus tavern) and Suetonius (narrative of emperors' lives subordinate to analysis of their personal hygiene), are often dismissed as not being 'proper' historians. Of course, if this comment *is* so interesting, why is it hidden down here in a note rather than being included in the main argument?

5. *P. Fam. Tebt.* 15, 19-21; *SB* xiv.11958; *P. Alex. Giss.* 43 = *SB* x.10651; *CPH = Stud. Pal.* v.66, 67; cf. the alternative (but unspecified, thereby giving the impression that it's not really worth worrying about) interpretation put forward by Kreuzfeld (1932), *contra* Jacoby, *ZPE* 3.7 (1894).

6. [Remember to insert more boring refs here]

7. Narratives include: R. Syme, *The Roman Revolution* (Oxford, 1939); H.H. Scullard, *From the Gracchi to Nero* (5th edn, London, 1982); P.A. Brunt, *Social Conflicts in the Roman Republic* (London, 1971); M.H. Crawford, *The Roman Republic* (London, 1978; 2nd edn 1992); M. Grant, *History of Rome* (London, 1978); T. Wiedemann, *Cicero and the End of the Roman Republic* (Bristol, 1994). Compare and contrast ....

8. Note that I am not talking about Holocaust denial, which attempts to explain away firmly-established facts (for which see D. Lipstadt, *Denying the Holocaust: the growing assault on truth and memory* [London, 1994]), but about different ways of representing what happened. See the articles in S. Friedlander, ed., *Probing the Limits of Representation: Nazism and the 'Final Solution'* (Cambridge, Mass., 1990).

9. D. Brown, *Bury my Heart at Wounded Knee: an Indian history of the American West* (1970).

10. 'The labours of these monarchs [Nerva, Trajan, Hadrian and the Antonines] were overpaid by the immense reward that inseparably waited on their success; by the honest pride of virtue, and by

the exquisite delight of beholding the general happiness of which
they were the authors. A just but melancholy reflection embittered,
however, the noblest of human enjoyments. They must often have
recollected the instability of a happiness which depended on the
character of a single man. The fatal moment was perhaps approaching, when some licentious youth, or some jealous tyrant,
would abuse, to the destruction, that absolute power which they
had exerted for the benefit, of their people. The ideal restraints of
the senate and the laws might serve to display the virtues, but could
never correct the vices, of the emperor. The military force was a
blind and irresistible instrument of oppression; and the corruption
of Roman manners would always supply flatterers eager to ap-
plaud, and ministers prepared to serve, the fear or the avarice, the
lust or the cruelty, of their masters.' Edward Gibbon, *The Decline
and Fall of the Roman Empire*, vol. I ch. III (ed. D. Womersley,
London, 1994, pp. 103-4).

11. For which see classics of feminist criticism like Simone de
Beauvoir, *The Second Sex* (London, 1953) or Germaine Greer, *The
Female Eunuch* (London, 1970).

12. 'Both experience and logic, then, suggest that the footnote
cannot carry out all the tasks that the manuals claim it does: no
accumulation of footnotes can prove that every statement in the
text rests on an unassailable mountain of attested facts. Footnotes
exist, rather, to perform two other functions. First, they persuade:
they convince the reader that the historian has done an acceptable
amount of work, enough to lie within the tolerances of the field
....Second, they indicate the chief sources that the historian has
actually used. Though footnotes usually do not explain the precise
course that the historian's interpretation of these texts has taken,
they often give the reader who is both critical and open-minded
enough hints to make it possible to work this out – in part.' A.
Grafton, *The Footnote: a curious history* (London, 1997), p. 22.

13. Perhaps also because of the teleology implied by the idea of a 'recipe' for history. On the other hand, we're quite happy, in other contexts, to talk of unpalatable decisions, not to mention tensions reaching boiling-point ....

CHAPTER 4

What is History *For*?

Pragmatism

Why study ancient history? It all depends, of course: who's asking the question, what sort of answer is expected, and what are the consequences if you get it wrong? Is it simply a question of trying to explain to some aged relative at Christmas what you're doing at university, where you risk only embarrassment, or are you having to justify the way you've spent the last few years of your life to a potential employer? The same answer will probably not serve for both, and, in the latter case at least, I doubt if you can afford to be completely open and honest in your answer. Very few people, I imagine, embarked on ancient history degrees with the express intention of becoming trainee supermarket managers – but, come the job interview, you're going to have to explain how your study of the Athenian *oikos* turns out to have been the perfect training for a career in retailing. If it's any consolation, your teachers are in more or less the same boat. Whatever their real views on the importance of ancient history (see them wince when you remark that you're doing it only because it seemed an easy way to get a degree), they too have to give the right sorts of answers when justifying their subject to people with power; above all the potential employers of their students, and (in Europe, at least) the agents of the state which funds university education and wants to make sure that taxpayers' money is being well spent.

Therefore, before thinking about why we actually find the study of the past interesting and important, we should consider briefly the sorts of answers that might be useful in our dealings with Them. In such situations we cannot afford to give the impression that the study of ancient history is a luxury, an enjoyable but basically unproductive way of passing the time. We need to show that the subject is useful, usefulness being understood almost exclusively in practical terms – above all, in economic terms. In the job interview, you must demonstrate how successfully your degree has trained you to take your place as a cog in the capitalist economy. Ancient history is clearly not a vocational subject like law or medicine; it is not a 'relevant' subject like economics, business studies or a modern language. However, it does teach a wide range of useful skills which can be transferred to other contexts rather than being 'subject-specific': the ability to process and analyse large quantities of information, to construct coherent arguments and develop ideas, to present arguments clearly and persuasively, to participate in discussion, and so forth. Ancient history teaches students to think critically and analytically; skills which are vital for understanding any subject, not just for thinking about the causes of the Peloponnesian War. Having established in this way that ancient history really is a practical and useful subject, you can now go on to emphasise the ways in which study of the past broadens the mind, deepens the understanding and enriches society in general.

You will be relieved to hear that these arguments usually do work, and ancient history graduates don't seem to find it any harder to get jobs than any other arts graduates. This is one justification for funding the teaching of ancient history at universities; there is a market for people with such skills. Another, equally pragmatic, argument emphasises the importance of the past (in the form of 'heritage') in the modern world; partly as evidence for a widespread interest in history, but above all because of its contribution to the economy. For example, tourism is now Britain's biggest earner of foreign currency, and the chief attraction of the country for foreign tourists is its past, marketed through museums, heritage centres and the like. Of course, the supply of people interested in working in museums greatly exceeds the number of jobs available, and many of those working in the 'heritage industry' have no training of any kind in history or archaeology (which are seen as less relevant than training in marketing and management). Moreover, there are plenty of reasons why, as historians, we might feel dubious about the sort of past being presented to the public in this way ('like burgers, in a convenient, instant and easily assimilable form') – but this just goes to show (we might argue) how great a need there is for the provision of proper historical training to help maintain this vital industry.

Finally, there is the supposed contribution of the study of history to social cohesion and stability. As a result of lengthy debate in the late 1980s, history (though not ancient history) gained a privileged place as a core subject in the National Curriculum for schools in England and Wales. The subject was seen, among other things, as a means of giving children a sense of identity and helping them to understand their cultural roots and shared inheritance. In American schools, history survives as part of civics, explicitly geared towards the inculcation of good citizenship. This does of course leave plenty of room for debate on what sort of good citizens we want; should children be taught a good dose of national history in the traditional manner, or should they be introduced to the histories of many different countries and cultures? The practical result, however, is a continuing demand for history teachers. Thus an obvious justification for funding history at university level is the need to train the teachers of the future.

History is seen to be useful and even relevant; this is the sort of answer that They want to hear, and we have little alternative but to give it to Them. I find it hard to believe, however, that these are actually the reasons why any of us is studying history. If this should ever become the case, the implications for the subject are devastating. If history is no more than a source of problems with which to test students' skills in analysis and information management, why should historians waste their time struggling to offer new perspectives on the past, rather than simply relying on tried and

tested material? If history exists simply to assist the marketing of the national heritage or to inculcate social values into
schoolchildren, what place is there for interpretations of the
past that aren't cosy, sanitised, easily marketed and socially
acceptable? I believe that all historians, lecturers and students
alike, will know instinctively that this would no longer be true
history; and hence that there is more to history than the
achievement of limited economic and social ends. The study
of the past may not be 'useful' in economic terms, but that is
not to say that it can be considered a luxury, either for
individuals or for society as a whole.

Looking to the future (1)

> It may well be that my history will seem less easy to read
> because of the absence in it of a romantic element. It will be
> enough for me, however, if these words of mine are judged
> useful by those who want to understand clearly the events
> which happened in the past and which (human nature being
> what it is) will, at some time or other and in much the same
> ways, be repeated in the future. My work is not a piece of
> writing designed to meet the taste of an immediate public,
> but was done as a possession for all time.
>
> Thucydides 1.22

Plenty of historians since Thucydides have offered this sort
of argument as a justification of their subject: history is useful
because knowledge about the past is useful in its own right.
Most obviously, we can argue that knowledge of the past is

essential for understanding the present, and clearly we want
to have the fullest possible understanding of the present
situation before making any decisions for the future. Many
advocates of history, however, would make far stronger
claims than this. By looking at what has happened in the past,
it is argued, we can draw conclusions about what is likely to
happen in future, and act accordingly.

The past shows us how people, or groups of people
(nations, classes, and so on), have tended to behave in a given
situation, so that we can anticipate their actions in similar
situations in the future. It shows us how institutions, political
or economic systems and even nations or whole civilisations
have tended to develop over time; once again, such knowledge enables us to anticipate events, either to take advantage
of them or to try to prevent them. The past shows us how
we should act in particular situations, to emulate the examples or avoid the mistakes of our predecessors. Study of the
past is even said to reveal the overall direction and meaning
of history, so that we can not only predict the likely course
of development of society for centuries to come but also live
our lives according to the moral or political principles which
are seen to be in harmony with this development.

How are we to evaluate such claims? Rather than looking
at the specific arguments of the different writers who claim
to be able to draw useful lessons from the past, I want to
approach this question by examining the assumptions common to all such attempts at learning from history. If these
assumptions seem plausible, we can go on to consider in

more detail the sorts of lessons we might learn from study of
the past. If not, we had better abandon the enterprise and
consider alternative justifications of our subject.

In the first place, all these approaches assume that the past
is a real object which we can study and against which we can
measure our conclusions. 'What really happened in the past'
is presented as the basis for conclusions about what will
happen in the future and what can and should be done about
it. It is also offered as the justification for a particular course
of action. Thus, for example, political parties analyse election
defeats in the hope of learning the lessons that will enable
them to win next time; Tony Blair concluded that the British
Labour Party had to abandon overtly socialist policies if it
was ever to regain power, while many Republicans interpreted Clinton's victories as a sign that their candidates had
not been assertive or right-wing enough. As we have seen,
however, we have no direct access to the 'real' past; what we
have instead are imaginative reconstructions of the past,
derived from historians' interpretations of the present traces
of past activity. Blair drew his conclusions not from 'what
really happened' in previous elections but from one interpretation of what happened. His opponents could easily offer an
alternative version of events which indicated a different
course of action in the present (and many still maintain
that Labour would have won the 1997 election on an old-
fashioned socialist platform).

Of course we believe that our understanding of the past is
superior to others', and hence that the lessons we draw from

it are the right ones. This isn't going to convince anyone who
doesn't, for whatever reason, agree with our interpretation of
the evidence. For example, non-Marxist historians often
argue that Marxists have not derived their conclusions about
the future development of society from study of the past but
have rather imposed their beliefs *on* the past. Marxists might
quite justifiably reply that the non-Marxists' reading of history is not (as it is presented) neutral and unbiased but simply
reflects *their* political agenda. In both cases, historians' interpretation of the evidence is inevitably affected by their
political beliefs. Neither camp has privileged access to the *real*
past, although both claim this in arguing that their predictions and prescriptions for society are correct. A more
sceptical view of historians' ability to show 'how it really was'
does not mean that we must give up attempts to learn from
the past, but simply that we have to accept the extent to
which our interpretations, and the conclusions we draw from
them, are subjective and provisional. We should certainly be
extremely suspicious of attempts to justify actions purely on
the grounds of their 'historical necessity' – that is, on nothing
more than a contested reading of an unstable, endlessly
rewritten past.

A second assumption, shared by many attempts to learn
lessons from history, is that past and present are sufficiently
similar to one another to make the comparison meaningful.
This assumption, and hence the use of historical arguments
in choosing a course of action, is most easily justified when
drawing on examples from the recent past. We should re-

member that Thucydides was studying what might be termed 'contemporary history', describing events which had taken place within living memory (not least his own). The usefulness of his account was based on the fact that things had not changed very much in the thirty-odd years since the war began. When he described the causes of *stasis*, civil war, at Corcyra in 427 BC (3.70-85), it was not a matter of merely 'historical' interest; similar conditions were still to be found in many Greek cities. Past and present clearly were comparable, and so Thucydides' account of what had happened could indeed offer important indications of what might happen in future. Once again, this line of thought can be clearly seen in the arguments put forward by Blair to the Labour Party: this is how the British electorate voted in 1992, and if nothing significant changes they will vote that way again, therefore you must accept these reforms. One way of responding to this sort of argument is to deny similarity. If circumstances have changed significantly, there is no reason to suppose that the historical comparison is relevant or that history will necessarily repeat itself.

This question of comparability becomes a much greater problem if we wish to make use of examples from more distant periods of history. It is easy enough to accept that events from the recent past *could* be relevant; it is not so obvious that a modern politician can learn anything useful from the politics of Victorian England, let alone from those of Republican Rome or Classical Athens. For this to be possible, it is necessary to assert that in some way political

activity is universal and unchanging, so that the thoughts of
Cicero, Demosthenes or Machiavelli on the subject can justifiably be taken out of their context and applied to
present-day situations. This principle holds true for any attempt to learn from the past. We have to assume some
measure of continuity between then and now, whether we
posit an unchanging national character (so that we can anticipate the likely behaviour of modern Germans by studying
German history over the past century or so) or an eternal
human nature (Elton: history teaches about 'man in relationship to other men'), or simply assert that a category such as
'war' or 'imperialism' or 'the economy' is universal, so that
evidence from past wars can be included unproblematically
in discussions of present emergencies. Certainly many military commanders over the centuries have tried to learn
lessons from historic battles, apparently on the grounds that
all military engagements can be studied purely in terms of
terrain, disposition of forces and so forth, abstracted entirely
from any historical context.

   This discussion may have called to mind my argument in
Chapter 2 about the use of modern theories and concepts in
studying the ancient evidence. There, too, we have to assume
some degree of similarity between past and present. Looking
at the past through the eyes of the present may suggest new
ways of reading the sources or making connections between
them, and so help us develop new interpretations of the past.
The reverse move may be equally productive; reading about
Athenian democracy may suggest new ways of thinking

about modern democracy (though probably through contrast as much as comparison). However, it is very rare that comparison allows us to assert that this is how it *must* have been in the past. The only examples which spring to mind are those which assume biological continuity between past and present and therefore argue that the findings of modern demographic or nutritional studies must be applicable to antiquity. Likewise, it is a gigantic step from suggesting that comparison with the past may be useful in thinking about the present to arguing that the past shows us how things will turn out in the future. At most, surely, the comparison may suggest one possible outcome or one possible course of action – and a brief survey of history will produce a range of other, equally plausible comparisons, suggesting quite different possibilities.

Looking to the future (2)

The alternative approach to learning lessons from history rejects wholeheartedly the idea that past and present are similar. Instead, it emphasises the differences between then and now, and seeks to explain how and why things have changed. If we can identify the underlying logic of historical development, the dynamics of change, the meaning of history as a whole, then we will be in a position to project this forwards and plot the future course of events. If we can recognise the shape of the story, we can have a fair idea of its likely ending. We are back in the realm of grand narratives and philosophies of history discussed in the last chapter. As I suggested, most 'proper' historians are highly suspicious of such narratives, and are often quite unconscious of their dependence on them for producing their own interpretations of the past. A few writers, however – Karl Marx is surely the most famous and influential – have set out quite explicitly to study the meaning and direction of history as a whole. They have tended to be equally explicit in the conclusions they draw from their studies about the future course of history and the lessons to be drawn from this.

For the sake of convenience, I suggest that we can identify three basic types of grand narrative. The first sees history as cyclical, an endless series of repetitions. A civilisation rises, prospers, declines and falls, and is succeeded by another civilisation which follows the same cycle: Sumer, Egypt, Babylon, Greece, Rome, Western Europe, America .... Once we have identified this cycle, we can try to locate our own position on it: is the West now in decline, as many twentieth-century pessimists have suggested? If so, is there anything that we can do to escape this seemingly inexorable process? This is by no means a new question; since the eighteenth century, writers have contemplated the awful spectacle of the Fall of Rome and debated whether the same symptoms of decadence and corruption were present in contemporary society. It is then a matter of opinion whether the study of history reveals to us an eternal cycle of repetition or a cycle which has simply not been broken *yet*; in other words, whether it is possible for us to diagnose the causes of the fall of civilisations and produce the necessary remedies to save our own society. Other versions of this kind of cyclical history suggest that revolutions always result in autocratic rule and/or the betrayal of their ideals, or that democracy inevitably degenerates into mob rule. This is clearly not a narrative for optimists or political radicals; it seems that the most we can ever hope to achieve is to prevent things from getting even worse.

Cyclical theories have never been very popular with historians. Some object to their determinism, the idea that individual actions are more or less irrelevant in comparison with the inexorable forces of historical development. Others point to the exceedingly cavalier use of evidence in every attempt to date at writing such an account of world history. The fundamental objection to a cyclical account, however, is that it makes a gesture towards taking account of historical change but in fact assumes an essential continuity over time. 'Civilisation', of which China, Greece, the United States and the Aztecs are all examples, is exactly the same, and follows the same laws of historical development, wherever it is found. Differences in technology, religion, ideas, economic and social structure, are all deemed to be irrelevant to the inexorable process of rise and fall. At best, it may be allowed that our society has a chance of escaping the eternal cycle, because we have at least succeeded in discerning the pattern of the decline of civilisations.

This does leave open the possibility that a cyclical view of historical change may still be useful when applied to a more restricted period of time and to just one aspect of society, where it may be less of a problem to assume continuity. For example, some economists make use of the idea of 'business cycles', or a cycle of 'boom and bust', as a guide to the future behaviour of the economy – but of course they take their evidence for this from the recent past, not from the economies of ancient Rome or sixteenth-century France. We may also need to take account of the influence of natural cycles like the passing of the seasons on human actions and behaviour and hence on historical developments. This is clearly a long way from saying that history as a whole is cyclical. Even if there was some tendency towards repetition, this would surely be negated by the attempts of people to learn from history and to prevent any such repetition. I see no reason to resist the temptation to quote Marx's classic observation on this subject, in *The Eighteenth Brumaire of Louis Bonaparte*: 'Hegel remarks somewhere that all facts and personages of great importance in world history occur, as it were, twice. He forgot to add: the first time as tragedy, the second as farce.'

Marx himself was one of the great exponents of the second variety of grand historical narrative, which represents the past in terms of a coherent line of development. Such accounts claim to have uncovered the hidden laws of historical change, which explain the past and can be projected into the future. Marx saw history in materialist terms, as the story of the development of the means of production (above all technology, but also legal institutions like private property) and the relations of production (slavery, serfdom, wage labour), the whole process being driven along by struggles between the different classes that make up society. Thus feudalism succeeded antiquity and was in turn succeeded by capitalism; in the future, capitalism too will be replaced by a society based on communism. Marx's survey of the past revealed that capitalism was not, as many of its apologists had assumed, universal and eternal. History proclaimed that a new form of society would in time inevitably come into being – and it also suggested ways in which people might act to bring this about sooner rather than later.

There are plenty of other versions of such linear narratives, attempts to discern the plot of the whole of human history. Christianity sees the workings of a divine plan which will culminate in the Second Coming and Last Judgement; however chaotic and meaningless events may seem, they all contribute to the ultimate fulfilment of God's will. The German philosopher Hegel saw the past in terms of the progress of human consciousness towards complete self-knowledge. Like Marxism, these narratives are teleological: history is seen to be moving towards a specific End which will be the culmination of all earlier developments. Other stories present this End as having already been achieved; arguing, for example, that the triumph of Western liberal-democratic capitalism over Soviet Communism means that the ideological struggles which had dominated history up to this point were now over. Narratives which concentrate instead on the development of technology and scientific knowledge reject the idea that history can have an end, since

society can always be transformed again by some new invention – unless somehow a civilisation might achieve absolute
knowledge and mastery of time and space (at which point,
according to most science fiction accounts, it tends to pass
onto a completely different plane of existence and leave the
field open to younger civilisations). Finally, we should mention the narratives of doom, which present human history in
terms of a sad decline from the idyllic world of hunter-
gatherer society (suggesting a future in which we have to
work ever harder and become yet more alienated from nature
and from our fellow human beings), or which see the entire
human race as bringing about environmental catastrophe on
a global scale.

If history really is about the fulfilment of the plans of an
omnipotent deity, it might seem perverse to try to oppose it.
Likewise, most of the other narratives imply that we should
ally ourselves with the progressive forces that will transform
society; 'history shows' that a particular development is both
progressive and inevitable, or even progressive *because* it is
inevitable. It is difficult to deny that many linear narratives
involve a certain amount of power worship, abasement before the inexorable forces of History. This is coupled with
the smug satisfaction that we are on the side that won
(western science and technology and liberal democracy rule!)
or that will win in the end (capitalism *will* be brought down
by class struggle or environmental forces or the Hand of
God). As I suggested above, I think (on political grounds, if
nothing else) that we should be enormously suspicious of

claims that a course of action is justified simply on the grounds of historical necessity.

How should we evaluate the claims of these narratives to explain the past and predict the future? One approach is to criticise them individually, on the grounds that their interpretations of the past are unconvincing and the actions they seek to justify are morally or politically objectionable. How does the Spanish Inquisition, staffed by men who were sincerely convinced that their actions would help bring about the Kingdom of God, fit into the divine plan? What of all the evidence that advances in technology have not actually made people happier or better-off? Can we really believe that the development of western science and rationality, which led directly to Hiroshima and Nagasaki, was entirely beneficial? A parallel tradition of opposition to such narratives is to offer alternative visions of the future: the dystopias of *1984*, *Brave New World*, *Planet of the Apes* and the like. Finally, one narrative may be opposed directly to another. Marx's theory has been criticised because he took no account of the possibility that in the future some new invention, which he could not predict, might transform society. Marxists might respond by arguing that the process of technological change is not independent of its social context; a capitalist society develops particular kinds of inventions, which have the capacity to transform society only when they are employed in the struggle between the dominant class and other classes.

The alternative approach to this question is to reject entirely the idea that there is any underlying logic or shape to

historical development. In place of a cyclical or linear narrative of history, we have the anti-narrative, which recognises
change over time but denies that it follows any coherent
pattern. Such a narrative may insist that historical development is more or less accidental; nothing can be learned from
the past, since it could just have easily been completely
different (if Cleopatra's nose had been longer, or Constantine
hadn't converted to Christianity, or Hitler had died in the
First World War ...). Events are seen to have causes, but
there is no over-riding Cause; there are no laws of historical
development. Human beings are seen to be free agents; their
actions may be influenced by forces of which they are not
conscious, but they are not determined by any such forces.

These ideas are usually presented as common sense, the
most obvious interpretation of human history, avoiding the
imposition of modern theories on the evidence. In fact, this
anti-narrative is no more or less a theory, a philosophy of
history, than Marxism or technological determinism. It simply offers a different story; one in which the past is presented
in satirical terms, emphasising the lack of order and meaning
in history. All we can learn from the past, according to this
view, is that the future is uncertain.

Understanding the present

It has to be admitted that history's record on prediction is
extremely poor; the obvious example being the complete
failure of anyone, Marxists and non-Marxists alike, to antici-

pate the fall of the Berlin Wall and the collapse of Soviet Communism. History is rather better at explaining what has happened – once the Wall had fallen, it was possible to look at the evidence of previous decades in a new light and to trace the roots of the crisis. As I've already suggested, history may be most useful in helping us to understand the present and the recent past, to see where we are and how we got here. We can then use this knowledge to help decide where we should go, rather than putting our faith in History to make the decisions for us.

I think it is fair to say that our knowledge of absolutely anything may be improved by looking at its history. At a fairly trivial level, it would be difficult to account for innumerable rituals and traditions, like the wearing of wigs in British law courts, the right of US citizens to carry weapons or the rules of cricket, without some reference to the origins of these customs. More importantly, studying the history of an institution can explain a great deal about the reasons why it has come to take a particular form and why it works in a particular way. For example, the complexities of the British constitution (not least the reason why there isn't a written constitution) need to be seen in the context of centuries of struggle between Crown and Parliament and between England and its neighbours. The constitution of the United States makes more sense when you consider the circumstances in which it was devised (the reasons why the colonists revolted, the influence of particular traditions of moral and political philosophy on their ideas) and its subsequent history.

More generally, we can try to understand our society by placing it in a wider historical context. At this point we can make a case for the relevance of *ancient* history, as well as the study of more contemporary periods. We can try to understand the present by comparing capitalism with earlier forms of society, or by comparing modern technology with earlier developments. In both cases, the example of the Roman Empire, a society that was highly organised and sophisticated but non-capitalist and pre-industrial, is clearly important. We need to consider modern democracy in the context of its ancient origins, since so many of the pioneers and theorists of democracy in the eighteenth and nineteenth centuries also looked to ancient political theory and institutions for inspiration and examples (although, interestingly, they normally preferred the example of the Roman Republic, essentially an oligarchy rather than a democracy, to that of Athens – which tells us something about the foundations of modern democracy). Of course, this historical perspective won't tell us everything we need to know, but simply looking at how society works in the present won't tell us everything either. Someone who concentrates too much on the past may forget that old traditions may take on new meanings and old institutions may work in new ways; in other words, what something was in the past is not necessarily a safe guide to what it is in the present. On the other hand, someone who concentrates too much on the present may fall prey to the equally misleading delusion that *this* is the natural state of things, ignoring the fact that it has been different in the past and will change in future.

History is important also because the past, or rather people's understanding of the past, shapes actions in the present. People do try to learn from the past, acting not only on the basis of their own experience but also the experiences of others. The past is seen to have authority, and thus plays a part in political debate: politicians and other leaders appeal to tradition and precedent in justifying their actions and in trying to win support for their policies (the classic British example being Margaret Thatcher's advocacy of 'Victorian values'). Further, past events provide motivation for present actions: nations go to war to avenge earlier defeats or to reclaim ancient rights, religious and ethnic groups remain locked in hereditary conflicts. It is impossible to comprehend the situation in Northern Ireland, or to understand what happened in the collapse of Yugoslavia, without bearing in mind how far the combatants are motivated by the thought of past atrocities and injustices perpetrated by the other side. Of course, these examples also point to the limitations of history. A historical perspective is essential for understanding how such conflicts arose and why they continue, but it offers no solution to them; it is in fact only when the different parties are prepared to let go of history and forget the past that peace becomes possible. If we look only at the past, there is a grave danger that we will conclude that the cycle of

violence is unbreakable, when it has simply not been broken
yet.

Above all, the past matters to people and so shapes their
actions because it is so important for their sense of identity.
'I' consists of a range of overlapping identities – for example,
in my case 'I' is male, white, middle class, English – each of
which is, to a very great extent, identified and defined by a
particular set of stories about the past. My sense of who I am
is in part based on my personal memories, on the stories I tell
(to myself and to others) about my own past. However,
consciously or unconsciously, I also identify with particular
groups (religious, political, social, ethnic etc.), each of which
offers its own set of stories about the past. Thus to be
English is to share (willingly or not) in a particular set of
stories about the Spanish Armada, Trafalgar, the Empire,
Dunkirk and the Blitz; to be American (or one sort of
American, anyway) is to remember the Mayflower and the
Alamo. Even simple dates have resonances: 1492, 1776,
1789, 1861, 1914, 1917, 1941, 1966, 1968. Of course I myself
have not experienced these events, but nevertheless the
memory of them shapes my attitudes and helps to define my
sense of who I am.

We are dealing here with historical myths, stories about the
past which make partial reference to something of collective
importance to the people who tell them. Myths not only
recount facts, they embody communal values, exemplify
virtues, offer warnings or lessons, legitimate practices or
institutions and even motivate actions. This is why politicians

are so keen on appealing to the past; they are trying to make use of the power of myth, the importance which certain stories hold for the people they wish to inspire, persuade or manipulate. In summoning up, say, the Dunkirk spirit, what's important is not what actually happened but what the story signifies for a particular audience (plucky little Britain, triumph in adversity, no surrender to Europe ...). Of course, these attempts don't always succeed, and may even backfire. 'Victorian values', for example, never really caught on in Britain; the myth appealed at best only to a narrow section of society, while most people had a far less positive view of Victorian society. However, it's easy enough to think of examples of the power of myth to determine people's actions. Protestants and Catholics in Northern Ireland define themselves in the present in terms of the past, each group offering a different account of Irish history. A celebration of an event like the Battle of the Boyne or the Easter Rising reinscribes and reinforces the identity of one group explicitly in terms of hostility to the other.

Changing the present

Myths are ubiquitous and indispensable; they tell us who we are, and help us make sense of the world. The historical perspective is useful because it allows us to see how people's attitudes and actions are shaped by their understanding of the past. However, history can also play a more active role: by changing people's ideas about the past, it affects their view of the present, and above all affects their sense of identity. This is the main point of George Orwell's nightmare vision of a society in which history is constantly rewritten to suit present circumstances and reinforce the power of the Party: 'Who controls the past controls the future: who controls the present controls the past.' As I suggested in the first chapter, this explains the ferocity of the struggle between history and other accounts of the past to be accepted as the authoritative version: the past matters to people.

History tends to undermine myth, by offering an account of the past that is consciously critical and founded more securely on the evidence. The power of a historical myth over its audience lies in the claim that it really happened, that it is not just a story. It also depends on the assumption that the meaning of the story is inherent in the events described. As historians we are likely to find ourselves emphasising that the myth offers just one of many possible interpretations of events: Dunkirk is not inherently a story of true British pluck, that is simply how the British have preferred to interpret it. We may also find that there are problems with the traditional version of events; for example, police reports of looting during the Blitz suggest that it was not true that 'we all pulled together'. In both cases, the historian's conclusions, deliberately or not, undermine these myths and reduce their power to inspire patriotism, courage and self-sacrifice. This raises some awkward questions. What right does the historian have to shatter people's illusions and unsettle their sense of identity? What right does the historian have to undermine the

existing social order, which is clearly to some extent rein-
forced and legitimated by these myths?

Myths provide comfort, security and a sense of identity for
some people, but they can also be enormously dangerous and
destructive. Too many myths provide a sense of identity for
one group at the expense of others. 'British' identity is too
often based on the suppression of distinctive Welsh, Scottish
and Irish identities – let alone the identities of those whose
ancestors came from the Indian subcontinent, Hong Kong
or the West Indies. The United States' search for a unified
and unifying 'American' identity is often seen as the imposition of WASP values and traditions on other groups:
African-Americans, Native Americans, Hispanics, Irish, Ital-
ians. Myths are used by politicians to justify harsh social
policies, violence, wars, persecutions, genocide. Hitler played
on German myths of natural superiority and national destiny,
and stories of Jewish plots and Jewish subhumanity under-
pinned the Holocaust. It is a positive duty for historians to
undermine the myths that are used to justify such actions. All
myths need to be criticised and, if necessary, opposed; it is,
perhaps, the only hope we have of changing people's attitudes and persuading them (rather than forcing them) to
change their behaviour.

Historians can oppose such myths by showing how un-
founded and implausible they are. More positively, they can
also offer alternative narratives of history. By offering different accounts of the past, we can to some extent rewrite the
present. Rumours of world-wide Jewish conspiracies and

atrocities need to be opposed with stories of the centuries of prejudice and persecution at the hands of Christians, and of the indispensable Jewish contribution to the development of our culture (not least the Jewish roots of Christianity). Likewise, the traditional account of the discovery of America relegates the original inhabitants of the continent to a minor role as savages who needed to be civilised. We may instead emphasise the high level of civilisation that existed before the Europeans arrived, and the savagery of the European conquest. Such 'revisionist' history may help to change the attitudes of the dominant groups in society, but it is most important for giving oppressed or excluded groups a sense of their own past and their own identity.

Stories about the ancient world play only a very minor part today in shaping national identities in the British Isles, let alone in America or other non-European countries. This cannot be said of Italy or Greece, though past greatness is not always seen in entirely positive terms; in the north of Italy, some people have started to identify with the Celts or the Lombards as an alternative to the Romans, to emphasise their wish for independence from Roman rule in the present. In the Balkans, debates about the 'Greekness' of the ancient Macedonians are intimately connected to the conflicts surrounding attempts to establish an independent Macedonia. However, the real importance of ancient history lies in the fact that the Greeks and Romans are seen as the founders of 'Western Civilisation' as a whole. Innumerable Western institutions, practices and attitudes have roots in the classical world, and claim authority in part because of their ancestry and long history – but this leaves them vulnerable to the effects of changes in our view of the classical past.

Ancient history can show how our culture has always been founded on oppression and exploitation, of women, slaves and the lower classes. It can show how classical civilisation had *its* roots in the Near East, thus opposing attempts to propagate myths of white European supremacy. Alternatively, the prestige of the ancient world can be used against the present day; for example, by showing how modern democracy is far inferior to its Athenian predecessor or by emphasising the comparative acceptance of homosexuality in Athens. We are forced to accept that the stories we tell about the origins of our culture are incomplete, inaccurate or misleading. In some cases, the intended lesson is that we should turn away from the past; in other cases, we are asked to try to live up to the example of the past which we claim to respect. Either way, historians have the opportunity to contribute to changing society – or, just as importantly, to help to resist certain changes – by offering alternative visions of society's past, and thus affecting our ideas of who we are and who we might become.

The fascination of the past

At any rate, this is how I justify to myself my decision to pursue ancient history as a profession rather than just a hobby: history is important, not only as an aid to under-

standing but as a force for change. This *still* doesn't wholly
answer the question why I, or others, find the past so fascinating in the first place. The past may be important to
people's sense of identity, but they don't all feel the same
urge to investigate it. As far as I know, no one has yet
conducted a survey to see what sorts of people are attracted
to history and what psychological peculiarities lead them to
become so interested in dead people and their affairs; we
simply know, usually from an early age, that the past intrigues
and allures us. It may take a psychologist, rather than a
historian, to say much more than that; but I would suggest
that at least part of the attraction is based on a strong feeling
of dissatisfaction.

In the first place, there is dissatisfaction with the identities
we are given and expected to adopt by parents, teachers and
society. Rather than accepting the traditional myths about
our past, we always wish to find out more; to seek out
alternative versions of events, to criticise the authorised
version. We reject the simple answers and refuse to take
things for granted because our sense of who we are is at odds
with what we are told we are. We know that appearances can
be deceptive, and that people's perceptions (of us, of anything) can be wrong. We will not let sleeping dogs lie. One
reading of the Greek myth of Oedipus suggests that the need
to uncover our true identity, whatever the consequences, is
an innate human characteristic. Perhaps historians are, unconsciously, convinced that they must be foundlings, and so
turn to the past in search of their 'real' parents.

In the second place, there is dissatisfaction with the present. Consider Elton's stated reason for studying history: 'The future is dark; the present burdensome; only the past bears contemplation'. Some people turn to history for comfort and reassurance, in search of a past that is less complicated and frightening than the present, more predictable and comprehensible. They seek out worlds which are more to their taste politically, spiritually, socially, culturally. This turn to history can simply be a means of escape, just as others try to deal with their sense of alienation (intrinsic to modern capitalist society) by embracing consumerism, soap operas, religion or other drugs. Plenty of historians seem to an extent to identify with, or even envy, the people they study. They are seen to have what we feel we lack, to be free from what we feel oppresses us. Their lives may have been shorter but they were more contented, more colourful, more refined and cultivated, more exciting, more ordered.

An interest in history may therefore reveal an inability to cope with living in the modern world. At the same time, however, the study of history may help us to understand the present and learn to live with it. One of the most disturbing qualities of modern life is the sheer pace of change and the instability and uncertainty this creates. History, which is interested above all in processes of change, may teach us how to come to terms with this. Moreover, history shows that things have not always been as they are now. It holds out the hope that, if we have problems with the world, the world can be changed.

Epilogue

It was, perhaps, a sense of dissatisfaction with the world in general and my allotted place in it that led me to history in the first place. My decision to write this book was certainly inspired by dissatisfaction, with the present state of ancient history – the books and articles that get published, the comments of reviewers, the way the subject is taught, the things that people say in seminars and conferences. I feel that the problems of historical theory and practice that have been worrying me – the problems I've discussed here – are far too important to ignore, and yet almost everyone seems to be ignoring them. The 'common sense' approach, in which the evidence is supposed to speak for itself with minimal interference from the historian, is largely taken for granted. Theory is treated as an optional extra, a marginal activity of interest only to eccentrics, rather than something which underlies *every* attempt at writing ancient history. Of course, if more ancient historians had been more interested in historical theory, it is unlikely that I would have had the opportunity to write this book.

My aim has been to raise questions about the way in which

we go about studying ancient history. I am not really worried about whether you have been persuaded by the tentative answers I have put forward, which probably seem dangerously radical and nihilistic from one perspective and pathetically cautious and wishy-washy from another. What matters is that you should have thought about the issues, and started to formulate your own response to them. If you now accept that these are questions which must be faced, this book has succeeded. Of course, I have higher hopes; that some at least of today's students will become tomorrow's *avant-garde* of ancient historians, sophisticated, theoretically aware and self-critical – and, with a bit of luck, more of tomorrow's ancient history will be not only scholarly but also interesting and even readable. An awareness of the issues raised by historical theory can surely only benefit the historian. It makes us aware of the limits set on our knowledge, certainly, but it also opens up great possibilities, suggesting new ways of thinking about the past and writing ancient history.

Further Reading

The most important question to ask about any bibliography is this: since it clearly does not contain everything that's ever been written on the subject, what's been left out and why? The optimist's view is that your teacher (who has of course read everything that's ever been written on the subject) has selected only the most important, relevant, clearly-written and generally helpful books, so as to save you from wasting time reading irrelevant rubbish. The more cynical might suggest instead that the selection consists almost entirely of books with which your teacher agrees, with just one or two others thrown in so that students can conclude that there *is* another side to the argument but it doesn't amount to much. Just to confuse things further, many teachers give extra credit for reading outside the prescribed bibliography – if it's worth reading, why wasn't it on the list in the first place?

General

The classic student texts on historical theory are for the most part rather old and very old-fashioned in their approach. The two most widely-read are E.H. Carr's *What is History?* (London, 1961; 2nd edn 1987), in its day quite radical and sceptical, and G.R. Elton's trenchantly conservative *The Practice of History* (Sydney, 1967). Neither are particularly recommended, except as historical curiosities: better to start with Keith Jenkins' *On 'What is History?'* (London, 1995), which summarises and discusses the ideas of both of them, as well as some more recent views. The most up-to-date, accessible and chatty introduction to contemporary ideas on historical theory is also by Jenkins: *Re-Thinking History* (London, 1991). For a response to the 'post-modern history' advocated by Jenkins, see R.J. Evans' *In Defence of History* (London, 1997). Other books worth reading are F. Stern, ed., *Varieties of History from Voltaire to the Present* (London, 2nd edn 1970), J. Tosh, *The Pursuit of History* (London, 2nd edn 1991) and M. Bentley, ed., *The Routledge Companion to Historiography* (London, 1997). Finally, I think all history students should read Hayden White's essay 'The burden of history', in *Tropics of Discourse* (Baltimore, 1978).

Chapter 1: What is History?

Many of the issues involved in the process of definition are examined by Jenkins in his two books (especially *On 'What is History?'*). The 'invention' of history by the Greeks is discussed in the introductions to the Penguin editions of Herodotus and Thucydides (by A.R. Burn and M.I. Finley respectively; both Harmondsworth, 1972). See also C.W.

Fornara, *The Nature of History in Ancient Greece and Rome* (Berkeley and Los Angeles, 1983), K. Dover, *Thucydides* (Oxford, 1973) and especially Paul Cartledge, *The Greeks: a portrait of self and others* (Oxford, 1993), ch. 2: 'Inventing the Past: history v. myth'.

Fiction: Paul Veyne's remark that 'history is a true novel' is found in the Prologue to *Writing History: essay on epistemology* (Manchester, 1984; French edn 1971), where, oddly, he claims that this statement 'seems innocuous'; Veyne's view of history is helpfully summarised in a review article by Peter Garnsey in *Journal of Roman Studies* 80 (1990), pp. 165-6. See also the first half of Hayden White's 'The fictions of factual representation', in *Tropics of Discourse*.

Myth: helpful introductions are G.S. Kirk, *Myth: its meaning and function in ancient and other cultures* (Cambridge, 1970) and *The Nature of Greek Myths* (Harmondsworth, 1974); Walter Burkert, *Structure and History in Greek Mythology and Ritual* (Berkeley, 1979). Martin Bernal's attack on nineteenth-century classicists is found in the first volume of *Black Athena: the Afro-Asiatic roots of classical civilisation* (London, 1987).

On history and science, R.G. Collingwood's *The Idea of History* (Oxford, 1946; 2nd edn 1993) is difficult but still stimulating; his definition of history as a kind of science is found in the Introduction. For rather stricter definitions, see A.F. Chalmers, *What Is This Thing Called Science?* (Milton Keynes, 1976) or G. Couvalis, *The Philosophy of Science* (London, 1997).

Examples of fringe or pseudo-history are legion. My

favourites are Erich von Däniken, *Chariots of the Gods? Was God an astronaut?* (London, 1969) and Iman Wilkens, *Where Troy Once Stood: the mystery of Homer's Iliad and Odyssey revealed* (London, 1990). Umberto Eco has enormous fun at their expense in his novel *Foucault's Pendulum* (London, 1989).

Chapter 2: The Use and Abuse of Sources

Among the many books designed to introduce you to the ancient sources and their problems (e.g. M. Crawford, ed., *Sources for Ancient History* (London, 1983)), it is possible to find one or two historians (not many more than two) discussing the problems inherent in the act of interpreting evidence. M.I. Finley wrote a number of articles on the subject, which can be found in *The Use and Abuse of History* (London, 1975; 2nd edn 1986) (especially 'Generalizations in ancient history', pp. 60-74) and *Ancient History: evidence and models* (London, 1985). Keith Hopkins provides an incisive critique of traditional approaches to ancient history in his review article 'Rules of evidence', *Journal of Roman Studies* 68 (1978), pp. 178-86, discussing Fergus Millar's *The Emperor in the Roman World* (London, 1977). Many of Hopkins' articles are exciting examples of how ancient history *could* be practised; see especially 'Taxes and trade in the Roman Empire', *Journal of Roman Studies* 70 (1980), pp. 35-77 (where he happily admits that his interpretation rests on a series of propositions which cannot be proved individually but which will support one another like a wigwam) and the two collections of 'Sociological Studies in Roman History', *Conquerors and Slaves* (Cambridge, 1978) and *Death and Renewal* (Cambridge, 1983).

For modern theories of translation, see George Steiner's monumental work *After Babel: aspects of language and translation* (Oxford, 1975; 3rd edn 1998), and Charles Martindale's discussion in *Redeeming the Text: Latin poetry and the hermeneutics of reception* (Cambridge, 1993), pp. 75-100, especially 85-92.

C. Vibius Postumus is found in the consul lists (*CIL* I^2 I = *Corpus Inscriptionum Latinarum* vol. I, 2nd edn, part I) and in the inscription from Larinum (*CIL* IX no. 730). Cicero mentions the family in his speech *Pro Cluentio*, sections 25 and 165. I got all this from Syme's *The Roman Revolution* (Oxford, 1939), pp. 362, 434, 436, 498.

Pecus and *pecunia* are discussed by the Roman writer Varro in *De Lingua Latina* ('About the Latin language') V.92 and 95, and *Rerum Rusticarum* ('Of rural things') II.1.11 (cf. II.1.9). Information on the nature of money in the ancient world can be found in C. Howgego, *Ancient History from Coins* (London, 1995) and S. von Reden, *Exchange in Ancient Greece* (London, 1995). The latter makes interesting use of anthropological models in studying ancient forms of exchange.

My source for the amphorae in the Saône was André Tchernia's article 'Italian wine in Gaul at the end of the Republic' in P. Garnsey, K. Hopkins and C.R. Whittaker, eds, *Trade in the Ancient Economy* (Cambridge, 1983), pp. 88-90. More information on the classification and interpretation of amphorae is provided by D.P.S. Peacock and D.F. Williams in *Amphorae and the Roman Economy* (London, 1986). Alternative interpretations of ancient trade are found in M.I. Finley *The Ancient Economy* (2nd edn, London, 1985), and Keith Hopkins' Introduction to *Trade in the Ancient Economy*, pp. ix-xxv.

Chapter 3: Telling the Story

The most prolific author on this subject is Hayden White. Rather than attempting to struggle through *Metahistory*, concentrate on the articles on 'Interpretation in history' and 'The historical text as literary artifact' in *Tropics of Discourse*; you might also look at some of the pieces in *The Content of the Form: narrative discourse and historical representation* (Baltimore, 1987), and Jenkins' discussion in *On 'What is History?'*.

As an introduction to contemporary ideas on literary theory, including narrative, voice, figurative language and other important topics, I highly recommend Andrew Bennett and Nicholas Royle's *An Introduction to Literature, Criticism and Theory: key critical concepts* (Hemel Hempstead, 1995). See also Italo Calvino's novel, *If On A Winter's Night A Traveller* (London, 1981).

Besides the books cited in the notes, the following might be useful and/or thought-provoking: on narrative, L. Stone, 'The return of narrative' in *The Past and the Present Revisited* (London, 1987), W. Martin, *Recent Theories of Narrative* (Ithaca, 1986), P. Brooks, *Reading for the Plot* (Cambridge, MA, 1984), especially chs 1-2, and A. Callinicos, *Theories and Narratives: reflections on the philosophy of history* (Cambridge, 1995); on voice,

J.P. Hallett & T. van Nortwick, eds, *Compromising Traditions: the personal voice in classical scholarship* (London, 1997), especially the papers by Charles Martindale, Susanna Morton Braund and Vanda Zajko; on rhetoric, A.J. Woodman, *Rhetoric in Classical Historiography* (London, 1988) and A. Grafton, *The Footnote: a curious history* (London, 1997).

Chapter 4: What is History For?

The threat to the place of history in British schools provoked a number of prominent historians to produce justifications of their subject, collected in J. Gardiner, ed., *The History Debate* (London, 1990). On the growth of the 'heritage industry' (also including interesting ideas about the importance of the past for people's sense of identity), see R. Hewison, *The Heritage Industry: Britain in a climate of decline* (London, 1987), K. Walsh, *The Representation of the Past* (London, 1992), P.J. Fowler, *The Past in Contemporary Society* (London, 1992) and above all D. Lowenthal, *The Heritage Crusade and the Spoils of History* (New York, 1996).

Elton deals with historical predictions, cyclical and linear narratives and the purpose of history in his usual style, pp. 56-69 of *The Practice of History*. Examples of a cyclical view of history can be found in Arnold J. Toynbee's collection of essays *Civilization on Trial* (Oxford, 1949), especially 'Does history repeat itself?' In *The Idea of History* (Oxford, 1946; 2nd edn 1993), R.G. Collingwood discusses the historical theories of Christianity (pp. 46-85), Hegel and Marx (113-26) and Toynbee (159-65), among others.

The bibliography on Marx's theory of history is enormous: try D. McLellan, *Marx* (*Fontana Modern Masters*: London, 1975), esp. pp. 38-49, then E.J. Hobsbawm, 'Karl Marx's theory of history' in R. Blackburn, ed., *Ideology in Social Science* (Glasgow, 1972), G.E.M. de Ste Croix, *The Class Struggle in the Ancient Greek World* (London, 1981), Part I, G.A. Cohen, *Karl Marx's Theory of History: a defence* (Princeton, 1978) or E.M. Wood, *Democracy Against Capitalism: renewing historical materialism* (Cambridge, 1995). A sustained attack (on the basis of the argument from technological progress) is found in Karl Popper, *The Poverty of Historicism* (London, 1957).

Examples of 'revisionist' history include: D.E. Stannard, *American Holocaust: the conquest of the New World* (Oxford, 1992); J. Wallach Scott, *Gender and the Politics of History* (New York, 1988), D. Halperin, *One Hundred Years of Homosexuality* (New York, 1990), D. Cohn-Sherbok, *The Crucified Jew: twenty centuries of Christian anti-Semitism* (London, 1992), Bernal's *Black Athena* (1987).

The only book I've come across so far that deals at any length with the psychology of historians and their interest in the past is K. Kearns' *Psychoanalysis, Historiography and Feminist Theory: the search for critical method* (Cambridge, 1997).

Index

Alamo, the, 154
alienation, 121, 161
anachronism, 80-1
archaeology, 66, 75
Aristotle, 28-9, 30, 65
Arthur, King, 19, 34
Athens, 37
Augustus, 76, 102, 106-7, 109
authority, 90-1, 112-14

beginning, 97-100
Bernal, Martin, 35, 38, 48
Blair, Tony, 139, 141
Blitz, the, 35, 154, 156
books, 64-5; boring books, 55, 78, 92, 93

Caesar, Julius, 59
Caligula, 119
capitalism, 134, 147, 148, 161
cats, Siamese, 9
China, 94, 145
Chinese Whispers, 64
Christianity, 65, 147, 149
Cicero, 65, 67, 71-2, 79, 80, 107, 142

Cleopatra's nose, 150
communism, 147, 151
conclusion, 128
conspiracy, 89, 92
context, 70, 80-1, 152
conversation, 115
cyclical history, 144-6

Decline and Fall of the Roman Empire, 42, 144
definition of history, 19-23, 27, 49-52
dissatisfaction, 160-1, 163
Dressel 1 amphorae, 69, 75, 86
Destiny, 35
dystopia, 149

economics, 28, 40, 41, 42, 45, 134, 137
economy, 85
economy, ancient, 88, 101, 102-3
Elton, Geoffrey, 99, 142, 161, 166
employers, employment, 133-5
environmental catastrophe, 148
escapism, 161
evolution, 58, 123-4

facts, 56-61, 69-71, 87-8, 93
fiction, 28-33, 54, 97-8, 123
Finley, M.I., 101, 102-3, 112
footnotes, 30, 32, 122, 128-31

Gibbon, Edward, 33, 116, 129-30

Hegel, G.W.F., 146, 147
heritage, 135, 137
Herodotus, 22, 24, 25, 26, 30, 33,
    63, 128
Holocaust, 59, 109, 129, 157
Hood, Robin, 34
'how it really was', 54, 57, 89, 94,
    97, 108, 114, 115, 139
Humpty Dumpty, 41

identity, 49, 154-5, 157, 158, 160
imagination, 31-2, 54, 84-6, 97
indifference, 13
inscriptions, 71, 72-3, 85
interpretation, 56, 57-8, 60, 62-3,
    68-9, 69-92, 94, 98, 104-5,
    107, 108

jam-making, 125
jargon, 120-2

Lampeter, 99
lessons from the past, 137-8,
    143-4
Livy, 100
Lucian, 11, 29, 38
luxury, 134, 137

Macedonia, 158
madness, 119
Manifest Destiny, 35
Marx, Karl; Marxism, Marxists,
    44, 48, 91, 140, 144, 146-7,
    149, 150
Mayflower, the, 35, 154
metaphor, 71, 12-5
money, 73, 77
myth, 33-8, 154-7

narrative, 90, 97-8, 100-11, 144-50
National Curriculum, 136
Northern Ireland, 153, 155
novels, 19, 29-30, 32

obfuscation, 120
objectivity, 62-4, 83-4, 89-90,
    91-2, 139-40
Oedipus, 160
oikos, 133
Orwell, George, 156
Ovid, 64, 65

pecunia, 69, 73, 77
pecus, 69, 73, 77
plot, 106, 109
poetry, 29, 33
polis, 74, 120
politics, 83-4, 91-2, 139, 141-2
Polybius, 63, 64
Postumus, C. Vibius, 69, 71-3,
    76, 78, 79
pragmatism, 134-6
prediction, 41-2, 43, 138-43

Procopius, 39-40
professors, 13, 90, 99, 112-13
propaganda, 38-40
Protestant Work Ethic, 103
psychoanalysis, 82
Pyramids, 46, 49, 85

racism, 35, 157
realism, 125-7
reality, 54, 57, 70, 125-6
revisionist history, 157-8, 159
revolution, 147
rhetoric, 26, 27, 39, 56-7, 70, 97,
    115-16, 116-18
Rostovtzeff, M.I., 83-4

Salamis, Battle of, 62-3, 68, 111
Sallust, 33, 38
science, 21, 40-5, 110, 122, 125
selection, 61-9
sexism, 91, 115-16, 159
shit, 120
silence, 67, 84-6
slavery, 31, 59-60, 102
solar system, heliocentric, 58
sources, 53-5, 61-6
students, 12, 55, 60, 87, 90-1,
    99-100, 102, 133-4
style, 29-31, 90, 97, 122, 125

surrealism, 125-6
Syme, Ronald, 76, 78, 86, 116

Tacitus, 33, 38
technology, 145, 147-8, 149
teleology, 147-8
Thatcher, Margaret, 153
theory, 79-82, 85, 94, 103-4, 142
Thucydides, 22, 23-8, 33-4, 35,
    36-7, 62, 100, 137, 141
titles, 98
tourism, 135
trade, 67, 79, 88-9
tragedy, 106-7, 109
translation, 72-4, 81-2
tyranny, 37

UFOs, 44, 49, 85, 89
Vesuvius, 53
voice, 111-16
von Däniken, Erich, 19, 46, 48-9
vulgarity, 120, 122

war, 142
Western Civilisation, 158-9
white middle-class males, 114-15
White, Hayden, 98, 105-6, 128

X-Files, The, 67